HERE'S WHAT PEOPLE ARE SAYING ABOUT
KIDS IN COMBAT AND THE MINISTRY
OF DAVID AND KATHIE WALTERS:

———————

I am nine years old. I attended a meeting
where David Walters ministered. It was
exciting. As we prayed I began to feel all
bubbly. It was as if I were a pot and the Holy
Spirit was boiling inside me. I spoke in
tongues for the first time. God is so good.
Joanna White
Abundant Life Community Church
Willimantic, Connecticut

David and Kathie Walters's approach to
children's ministry is a fresh wind blowing
in an area that is critical to the church.
The effectiveness of their strategy has to do
with equipping children to minister,
rather than viewing children as objects
of ministry. I highly recommend them.
Jim Jackson, president
Christian Believers United
Montreat, North Carolina

David Walters is a mighty father of faith
to this generation of children. His book
Kids in Combat gives pastors, youth leaders
and parents a great instruction manual on
how to equip children for spiritual war.
Bob Perry, youth minister
New Covenant Fellowship
Manassas, Virginia

One of the most significant, essential tools for the church of the nineties and her children...It will revolutionize how children are viewed and taught, consequently activating them in the gifts of the Spirit, intercession and warfare.

Esther Ilnisky, founder
Esther Network International
West Palm Beach, Florida

Since the Walters seminar, our junior church is so exciting. Each time we meet, God touches us with visions, words of knowledge and all the wonderful gifts Jesus has prepared for us.

Chris Galle, youth minister
The Worship Center
Hebron, Connecticut

Kids in Combat speaks about the reality of the Holy Spirit in the lives of youth and children. In my own church, I've been thrilled to see the Spirit move in our children's meetings in ways we had only expected in the adult service.

Bob Foss, associate pastor
Vineyard Christian Fellowship
Bakersfield, California

Kids in Combat is excellent. I stayed up until the early hours of the morning to finish reading it, thinking that I would just read the first few pages before going to sleep. I could not put it down.

Jenny Elliott
Sozo Fellowship
Hampshire, England

We have been conducting weekly meetings for our eight- to thirteen-year-olds since David and Kathie Walters had a seminar in our area. A friend of mine came to the house during one meeting looking visibly ill. After the children prayed for her, she was instantly healed. My twelve-year-old son also gave her an accurate prophetic word about her walk with the Lord.

Matt and Ingrid Metell, pastors
Harvest Light Christian Center
North Windham, Connecticut

During a seminar, David Walters and the children ministered to my three-year-old son, who suffered brain damage due to a swimming accident. His improvement in the next two weeks astonished the doctors. My husband also accepted the Lord that weekend, and my twelve-year-old son was speaking in tongues. It was a great experience for our entire family. (And my children are still mighty warriors in God's army!)

Wanda Kelly
Harvest Lake Christian Center
Ellington, Connecticut

Kids
IN COMBAT

*Training Children
and Youth to Be
Powerful for God*

DAVID WALTERS

**CREATION
HOUSE**
BOOKS ABOUT SPIRIT-LED LIVING
LAKE MARY, FLORIDA

Creation House
Strang Communications Company
190 North Westmonte Drive
Altamonte Springs, FL 32714
(407) 862-7565

OTHER TITLES BY DAVID WALTERS:

The Armor of God
A children's Bible study based on
Ephesians 6:10-18 (illustrated)

Fact or Fantasy
A study on Christian apologetics
designed for children (illustrated)

Equipping the Younger Saints
A guide for teaching children
about spiritual gifts

ACKNOWLEDGMENTS

We would like to express our gratitude to several friends who have helped to make this book possible:

• To Lee Grady for his time in editing and preparing the original manuscript for publication and to Judy Gilbert for her time in preparing and editing the revised edition.

• To all the many parents, youth pastors and children's workers who have asked questions about children's ministry — we offer a special thank-you for provoking us to seek the Lord for His answers!

• To all those fellow ministers who offered their input and critique for the second edition.

• To Stephen Strang, Walter Walker and the staff members of Creation House and CharismaLife who were excited about our vision for children and youth. Their excitement has been transformed into this new, expanded version of *Kids in Combat*.

CONTENTS

PREFACE

I f we have learned one thing during our years of ministry, it is this: Nothing works without the power of the Holy Spirit. Before you as a leader can focus on guiding children or young people, you must be willing to see the Holy Spirit work in your life and your church.

Kathie and I experienced this firsthand as we were introduced to the Holy Spirit in the late 1960s. Prior to this experience we sat for ten years under the ministry of a very famous expository preacher, Martyn Lloyd-Jones, pastor of Westminster Chapel in London, England. Our grounding in the Word of God went beyond the boundaries of what most people receive, and we praise God for this foundation in our lives.

This wonderful and precious man of God taught on the book of Romans for ten years and the book of Ephesians for six. If ever there was a dedication to the teaching of truth, it was in this man. He also taught on the baptism of the Holy Spirit, and when we received it he encouraged us to "go on." He felt that it was his job to take us to Jordan, as it were, but that we must now pass over. What a humble man! How many teachers and preachers today can freely acknowledge the limitations of their ministries to this degree?

As we moved further in our understanding of the Holy Spirit's ministry, we became a part of a tremendous revival in the south of London in 1969. We had no personal experience with the gifts and the moving of the Holy Spirit, only the teaching from Dr. Lloyd-Jones. We didn't even know that God would actually speak to us except through the Bible. We had to depend entirely upon the Spirit to teach us.

People somehow began arriving at our home from all over the area (and some from long distances away), and all of them were seeking something from God. All we could do was let God do what He wanted to do. We simply gathered together to worship. Jesus was our only central theme, and the reality of His presence was all that we were seeking.

We were not interested in more teaching. Nearly every one of us had received enough teaching to live out for twenty-five years! Between seventy and eighty people crammed into our little duplex three times a week. Whenever two or three happened to meet anywhere, a spontaneous meeting resulted as well. As we worshipped the Lord, the Holy Spirit would arrive and take over.

No one led the meetings; no one else had pre-eminence. There was no special form or pattern; we had no agenda or program. No two meetings were alike (except for special teaching meetings which came later.) We never knew what was going to happen, and we never had any idea when the meeting would end. The power of God washed our minds of the unnecessary religious traditions and nonessential doctrinal concerns.

The Holy Spirit also revealed to us that Jesus Christ was a Person and not a doctrine. After singing two or three worship songs, it was common for twenty or thirty people to fall to the floor as the presence of the Lord filled the room. Sometimes when the Holy Spirit ministered to us, everyone would break down and weep. The glory of God would be evident on each face.

At other times the meetings would be nothing but laughter as a spirit of victory was poured out. People would lie on the floor and laugh for hours. All our religious bondage was washed away.

After a while there were too many people to meet in the house, and we moved our main meeting to the local town hall. We would sometimes arrive at the meeting and have to step over people lying outside the entrance because the Spirit had already come upon them as they were entering the hall.

Our meetings were seldom led from the pulpit. We actually had no "front," no platform or worship leader to tell us to stand up, clap, sing or shout. The Holy Spirit orchestrated the meetings, and we simply learned to be led by the Spirit. Jesus was the director. How marvelous that He is able to do that!

Of course, there were elders whom God raised

up, but they did not feel duty-bound to run the meetings. They simply cared for the flock, gave spiritual oversight and encouraged the people to discern for themselves.

The people in that revival had a spiritual discernment like no other people we have ever met. Why? Because they didn't depend on a few people to shoulder the responsibility. They trusted the great Shepherd. They all knew He could take care of His own. Therefore, they simply ministered to the Lord as the Spirit led them.

As a challenge, it would be good for us to examine our current ideas on how our church meetings should be conducted. Kathie and I have been in hundreds of services in different churches throughout the United States. Many of them have been so similar that we wondered if they were all using the same handbook.

When we were in a church before we were filled with the Spirit, we were always served what was called the "hymn sandwich." All the churches offered the same menu: a hymn, a prayer, another hymn, some announcements, a hymn, a sermon, a prayer, a closing hymn and a benediction. After we became Spirit-filled, we assumed that all Spirit-filled churches were Spirit-led. We did not realize that many simply have another form of the hymn sandwich.

The meetings usually consist of three or four lively songs, each interrupted by pep talks from the worship leader or pastor, often with the sound system set at a deafening level so that the congregation is intimidated by the microphones. This is then followed by two or three worship songs with little or no waiting on God for the gifts of the

Spirit to flow. Then there might be a special song, an offering, some announcements and a message. The people are often merely spectators rather than participants, listening to one or two leaders give an exhortation rather than the body members "exhorting one another" (Heb. 10:25).

This is not to say that pulpit ministry is wrong or that we never need a platform. But if only the leaders minister, then the body will never be able to function, the children will be neglected and the Holy Spirit will be quenched (1 Thess. 5:19). We are definitely not suggesting that a spirit of anarchy should prevail, for we firmly believe in correct spiritual oversight and delegated authority. However, a little more trusting in the sovereignty of the Holy Spirit in the meetings would really bring about desired breakthroughs.

However, it is not enough for our meetings to be good. We are not merely to seek that which is good but that which is of God. We can accept that which is good and miss God altogether. A good song, a good testimony, even a good message can stop the flow of what God is doing or saying at the time.

Our question is this: If the adults do not move in the Spirit during their church meetings, how will the children learn to do so?

The purpose of this book is twofold: 1) to bring churches and church leaders back into Spirit-empowered ministry and 2) to pass that power on to our children. We do not want to experience the same thing that happened to Joshua's generation: "And there arose another generation after them, which knew not the Lord, nor yet the works which he had done for Israel" (Judg. 2:10).

INTRODUCTION

As we have traveled throughout the body of Christ in the United States, we have been concerned by what we have seen. Where the ministry of the Holy Spirit has been cast aside, the children and the youth also suffer. To think that organization and programs can replace the presence of Christ in a congregation!

Jesus is the One who is to have pre-eminence. When He is in our midst, He will minister to every need. The Holy Spirit uses all kinds of vessels when there is an openness to receive from God. His power can be manifested through whomever He chooses to move at the time — including children.

We have many experiences to tell about how God moved during the revival in the south of London in 1969. But we noticed one important thing that was always obvious: God never left out the children and the young people. They were used just as powerfully as anyone else, both inside and outside the meetings. Often children would speak prophetic words, and the Holy Spirit would come upon them as they ministered in power. Some of the children were responsible for revivals in the state schools that took place as a result of their preaching to and praying for other children.

We mention other movements of the Holy Spirit in this book, but the point we are trying to make is simple: In the Spirit, there is no Jew or Greek, black or white, young or old. The Holy Spirit can move in a remarkable way through the children and the young people. But we must acknowledge that God can do this and make room for them.

That is why my wife, Kathie, and I have spent the past twenty years traveling and speaking about the anointing of God to children and young adults, Sunday school teachers and youth pastors. When we minister, we expect — and see — children age six or younger receive the Holy Spirit and begin to exercise gifts of the Spirit.

We often meet people who tell us they would like to see the children and youth continue to move in the church meetings in the same way they did when we were there ministering. So often that does not seem to happen after we leave. Unless the leaders encourage the whole church — including the youngsters — in their spiritual potential and make a way for them to participate in the meetings, it will not generally happen. Many times the children are stuck in the back of the church meeting, which encourages them to "phase out." When I preach in churches, I usually have them come down to the front, and I get them involved in the message.

Many pastors preach wonderful sermons to the congregation but do not involve or include the children in the message, even though they may be present. This encourages the children to think the pastor is only talking to their parents, so they tend to phase out. The pastor must address the children from time to time and tell them that they are members of the church also and that God thinks they are important.

If you want to make room for God, you must make room for the children. God wants to use them. They are not full of doctrines, and they are not initially pretenders when it comes to church. They love to see God move, and they don't pretend He's there when He isn't.

What we are sharing in this book is not just a theory about children's ministry or a scriptural revelation. It is based on what we have seen God do with children and what we continue to see Him do everywhere we travel. By excluding the children we can exclude a move of the Spirit. But by acknowledging that God will use these little ones, we take a blow to our pride, and there is more room for God!

Another part of the reason for writing this book is to address common problems with youngsters before they happen. Several years ago when we were witnessing to street prostitutes in a city in Florida, we found that a large number of teenage girls who were on the streets had been raised in Pentecostal denominations.

Many ministries have been organized to help these youngsters after they have fallen. I have experienced these ministries, preaching in juvenile detention centers, halfway houses and street coffee houses. Yet I am convinced that prevention is better than cure. As someone once said, "A fence at the top of the cliff is better than an ambulance service at the bottom." We understand how children who have no religious background can end up in these places, but it troubles us to see a Christian child do the same thing.

The leading children's minister in England, Ian Smale (known as Ishmael), told me that 80 percent of all church-raised kids have nothing more to do with church when they become young adults. If this is correct, then we need to break that trend.

This book gives some ways to keep children who are raised in the church from turning to the world. But, more important, it will give you principles and guidelines that will help to raise up an army of young people for God. It is designed as a handbook for parents, youth pastors, Sunday school teachers and children's workers.

Our book does not cover all aspects of ministry to children and youth. In the areas of physical, emotional and sexual development or education, we have limited our input. It is not possible to cover all of these aspects, and it would be foolish for us to comment at length on topics in which we do not have complete expertise.

In the fields of child and youth evangelism, however, this material is not merely theoretical. We have practiced it over many years. When these principles are coupled with a reliance on the Holy Spirit, the young people you work with will experience the life-changing power of God.

CHAPTER ONE

A VISION FOR YOUNG PEOPLE

Imagine for a moment a large army of adults standing in ranks, prepared for battle. Behind them, looking rather uninvolved and complacent, is a scattered group of children and teenagers. Although the adults seem ready to fight, the children behind them look totally unprepared and disinterested.

This is an actual vision which we received several years ago regarding the state of the church. In the typical church today children are pushed to the back of all our programs and activities. They are sent off to children's church to be entertained while the adults receive from the Word and learn to walk in the Spirit. Why is this?

In the vision that we received the adults were so busy trying to find their own ministries that they actually jostled the children and teens to the back. Also, the majority of the adults in the army did not believe that children were of any real spiritual significance. But then we saw God's hand come down from above and part the ranks of adult soldiers. His right hand came behind the children and drew them forward into the ranks with the adults. We then heard the Lord speak to us that His Spirit was just as mighty in these youngsters as He is in anyone else.

From this vision we can conclude that children do not have a "baby" or "junior" version of the Holy Spirit. He is the same age in them as He is in us. Even though they may be young, immature and inexperienced, God's Holy Spirit working in them *is* the power of God.

We also had a similar vision in which the children in militant countries were compared to the children in America's churches. The youngsters we saw in the militant countries were being trained in combat with weapons. They were marching in rank and file, and some were being taught the principles of Marxism while others learned the tenets of militant Islam. They were giving themselves wholeheartedly to the goal of world domination.

But the children we saw in America's churches were only playing. They were giving themselves to entertainment and were totally unprepared for spiritual warfare. We then heard the voice of the Lord, saying, "Satan is preparing his army, but My church is entertaining her children." In the next scene we saw children and teenagers in different rooms being trained in the truths of God's Word. They were being taught how to intercede in prayer, evangelize and move in the power of God.

What we desperately need is a radical departure from the standard method of children's ministry in the church today. Much of the material in this manual may seem revolutionary. That's because it is so different from the way children's ministry is conducted in the average church.

If you are not open to change and are satisfied with the way your programs for children and youth are being carried out now, then read no more! But if you are concerned about the lack of vision, power and commitment in your children and teens, not to mention the adults in your church, then please continue.

Be prepared to lay aside old traditions and move in faith, expecting that God can and will radically change your church's vision.

The Role of the Church

Children and teenagers typically have been neglected in many churches. Although a great deal of time and money has been devoted to provide materials and programs for them, most of this has resulted in pathetic results. What is the problem?

We need to understand that born-again children are brothers and sisters in the Lord first and children second. They are not just cute and bothersome little creatures whom we simply herd off into a back room after the praise and worship service — only to be given to an enthusiastic teenager or a dedicated mother for babysitting.

Telling stories about Daniel in the lions' den or Jonah and the whale can quickly become boring after the seventh retelling. Yet this is what we normally give our children when they come to a church meeting. There is nothing wrong with enthusiastic teenagers or dedicated mothers being involved in teaching children, but it should not be at the expense of the apostolic ministry. Our children need to hear the Word of God coming in power just as the adults expect to hear it each time the church gathers together!

So much of children's ministry has been left to the women, yet there is no scriptural foundation for this. We suspect that many Christian men feel it is beneath them to become involved with children.

Much emphasis has been made in recent years on the parents' responsibility to train their children. This has been excellent, considering the great need to restore the family in this country. Some years ago at a pastors' seminar in Florida, a Bible teacher even suggested that children's and youth ministries are unscriptural because parents are responsible for training the children.

We agree that the parents must be more active in their children's spiritual development than just dropping them off at church. As that teacher suggested, the church leadership can't take sole responsibility for training children. However, I believe the church still needs to perfect and equip children for God's service through the five-fold ministry of apostles, prophets, evangelists, pastors and teachers (Eph. 4:11-12).

If training were only the parents' responsibility, then by the same logic we as adults should not have been taught by the church ministries but only by our parents! Our children need to be in church and hear the Word of God preached in power. They need to see and participate in the moving of the Holy Spirit. They need to have a sense of destiny and feel a part of what is happening in the body of Christ. They need to understand the supernatural and prophetic elements that have brought their own local church into being.

One church in Kansas City, Missouri, has a three-day feast every year in which their church history is recounted. The children in attendance come to know the awesomeness of God and how wonderfully He has dealt with the church, both individually and corporately, over the years.

Unfortunately, many local churches have no sense of a supernatural personal history, perhaps because someone had just thought it would be good to start a church. If that is the case in many churches, then there is nothing to pass on to the children that would motivate them to become a part of God's mighty purpose.

The Scriptures record how the children of Israel were instructed to explain to their children God's historic dealings. Therefore, their children could pass on a sense of destiny that would, in turn, affect their own children's lives (Deut. 6:20-25; Josh. 4:5-7, 19-24; Ps. 78:1-8).

When I first began preaching in churches, the children would often be taken out of the service just before I began my message. "Why are you doing this?" I would ask. "I want to preach to them, too." Usually the answer would be, "We have a special curriculum or children's program for them." At other times we would be given the children, but the adults would leave the meeting. "You are missing it again," I protested. "You are hearing, but you don't perceive!"

When Jesus met with the multitudes, can you imagine Him saying to Peter, "Go and arrange for some of the women to take the children out for children's church before I begin to minister"? Of course not! Jesus, the great Shepherd of the sheep, is the One who said, "Suffer the little children to come unto Me and forbid them not." Yet today, many undershepherds in the church are saying, "I am not called to minister to children. Let the women do that."

The Bible says:

> They brought unto Him also infants that He would touch them: but when His disciples saw it, they rebuked them. But Jesus called them unto Him, and said, "Suffer little children to come unto me, and forbid them not: for of such is the kingdom of God. Verily I say unto you, Whosoever shall not receive the kingdom of God as a little child shall in no wise enter therein" (Luke 18:16-17).

It has been our experience that if you can successfully minister to children, then you can minister to anyone!

What We Should Expect

We live in a hedonistic society. For many children and adults, fun is the name of the game. We are told that we should give the children lots of fun activities to keep them interested. We are also told to make the church a fun place to be.

Even though children's organized recreational

time should have spiritual truth built into it, some churches go so far as to do all their spiritual teaching for children with the means of visual media and entertainment: puppets, clowns, videos, crafts, cowboys, pirates, mime, etc. These methods may be fine as a secondary emphasis but should never be the main course.

Many of our children spend most of their waking hours in recreation. "If I can just get through my schoolwork, I can go and play" — that is the common lament of so many children. Work or learning has become a dirty word to them.

Secular and even Christian schools are now taking the children away from us. In the past, schools were designed to teach only the basics. But today parents spend six days a week providing a taxi service for their children, transporting them to the social activities conducted by the schools. This is simply another subtle way to destroy God's divine order for the family.

Our children are being influenced by peer pressures outside the home, and the parents are losing the children to the system. Children who spend unlimited time among their own peers will be adversely affected. As Proverbs 22:15 says, "Foolishness is bound in the heart of a child." The sin nature is like the law of gravity; it has a downward tendency. If we simply leave our children to their own devices, they will naturally develop in their sin.

Children are not born innocent. The Adamic nature is their inheritance. They may be innocent about the different ways of sinning, but you can be sure that their nature is to sin. Psalm 51:5 says, "Behold, I was shapen in iniquity; and in sin did my mother conceive me." I have yet to meet a parent who is frustrated because his or her child refuses to disobey. It is always the other way around! We invest all our energy in training them to obey. We never have to train them to disobey. That comes naturally.

Many children are programmed to obey their elders as a last resort:

> "Clean your room, Jimmy!"
> "OK, Mom."
> Ten minutes later: "Jimmy, I told you to clean your room."
> "I am, Mom." (Then he thinks, "When I get to it....")
> Ten minutes later the parent resorts to exaggeration: "If I've told you once, I've told you a thousand times: Clean your room!"
> "Mom! I am going to do it right now!"

Ten minutes later the room is still not cleaned, and Mom is usually shouting at this point.

Now that Jimmy has his mother worked up and at her nerves' end, he's about ready to obey. He has learned over the years that she really means what she says only when she is screaming. We need to teach our kids that obedience is only obedience if it is instant. When God tells us to obey, He means it. He doesn't lie to us the first two or three times. We must treat our youngsters the same way.

However, some children today don't receive guidelines from their parents at all. When I was a child and we visited someone else's house, we were only allowed to go into designated areas such as the playroom or the backyard. I notice that today many children will come with their parents to someone's house and then just take off and run everywhere. The hosts often have to put up with small children running in and out of their bedrooms and grabbing hold of ornaments and antiques.

Are our children too young for us to expect much from them? Do we have to wait a number of years for them to have their own relationship with God? If children do not possess real faith in Christ for themselves but just an inherited belief from their parents and teachers, then you can be sure that they will eventually be influenced by other modes of thought in the world.

Many parents today are devastated because their teenage children have fallen into the realm of sex and drugs, even though they were raised in the church. The parents cannot understand what went wrong. It's simple! The children easily adopted new peers because they never had a real encounter with Christ the Son of God.

Children Can Have a Solid Foundation of Faith

Our children and teens need to know God in such a way that if their parents stopped believing or if their friends stopped believing or even if their pastor became backslidden, their faith would stay strong. Their confession and experience must be: "I know whom I have believed, and am persuaded that he is able to keep that which I have committed unto him against that day" (2

Tim. 1:12).

Years ago Christians used to talk about "saving faith." They were not content just to hear someone profess he was a believer or that he had faith. They were concerned that an individual possessed faith to the saving of their souls. We need more of this concern today, and we need to teach it to our children.

In Paul's letter to the Galatians he talks about being kept under the law, shut away from faith until it was later revealed (Gal. 3:23-26). He discusses the fact that the law was a "schoolmaster" to bring mankind to Christ. In the same way, outward pressure is the main reason many of our children stay in line, even though they profess faith. Because of their immaturity, they need a schoolmaster (outward force) to keep them disciplined. Therefore, as they get older, a number of them rebel and reject Christianity altogether.

Paul says in Galatians, "After that faith is come, we are no longer under a schoolmaster" (v. 25). Could it be that faith has never come for many of our youngsters? The true, saving faith that the old saints talked about is not being experienced by many of our youngsters. They simply give the gospel their mental assent, which quickly dissipates when the pressure is on. Mental assent is destined to fail. And when it does, they become disillusioned and head straight for the world.

Pressure on the outside from religious adults or peers may have a purpose, but it is only temporary. *Inner* pressure from the Holy Spirit is the force that will change our youngsters! The Holy Spirit, warring against the flesh from within, is going to get the job done (Gal. 5:16-18). Our children are going to be triumphant when they really see the power of Christ in the believer and seek to experience saving faith. Then they will no longer be content to simply please others.

This does not mean that spiritually disciplining our children is of no value. I have been alarmed when on several occasions mothers have said to me, "I wish my child was here attending your meetings. It would be so good for him [or her], but he did not want to come." When I have asked, "How old is the child?," the ages have been between nine and fourteen years. Since when has a child made his own decisions about attending church? We do not give them choices regarding attending school, brushing their teeth, taking a shower or eating their vegetables.

It seems that some parents have no problem in disciplining their children except in spiritual things. Think about the scriptural injunction in Proverbs 22:6, "Train up a child in the way he should go: and when he is old, he will not depart from it." That means simply that a child is under the parents' authority as long as he or she lives under the same roof and is dependent on them, regardless of age. The word *old* could also be read as *independent*.

Another implication of Proverbs 22:6 is that parents are expected to help their children taste the things of God (like feeding nourishment to an infant). A child who has tasted God will serve Him from internal motivation rather than from external pressure. However, in the same way that children sometimes need encouragement to eat, they sometimes need encouragement to taste of the Lord.

For example, some children may be compelled by their parents to attend the church services, but they still refuse to enter into the spirit of the meeting, especially during praise and worship. During this time they may sit there glumly with a rebellious attitude. Parents must be careful not to allow this to continue. The way to deal with this is not to let them just sit there but to insist they enter into worship.

Evelyn Hamon, the wife of Bill Hamon of Christian International, relates how she had communicated to her children that they as a family were committed to serve the Lord. Her four children attended all the meetings and were encouraged to enter into worship. If they refused to raise their hands during praise and worship, she would pinch them under the elbows. Their hands would go up, and tears would come to their eyes. The people would say, "Look at the anointing on those children," but it wasn't the anointing. They were in pain!

Regardless of what many people may think, this religious discipline did not make the children grow up hating God and leaving the church. Rather, all of them are now involved in full-time ministry.

When I was a young Christian many years ago, I was always struggling to have the victory over the desires of the flesh. I believed that if I could accomplish a victory over my passions, then I would be qualified to walk in the Spirit. It took a long time for the Holy Spirit to show me that as I walked in the Spirit through active faith, I would not fulfill the desires of the flesh. There is no reason why our children and teenagers cannot have the same active, saving faith — a faith which is not from human origin, but divine!

But What About the Small Children?

Many people ask us about very small children and how they can be expected to experience the Holy Spirit or participate in church services. I share with them what I saw in a church in Tabb, Virginia, formerly pastored by Judson Cornwall (now pastored by Chuck and Betty Call). This church goes into deep worship at each gathering, and I have been astounded to see little children and toddlers worshipping on their faces while bowed before the Lord. The last time I was there I did not see one child running around or hear one infant cry during the entire meeting.

I asked the pastor's wife for their secret. "It's very simple," she related. "When new parents come to a service with a small child who starts to act up or make noise, we encourage either of them to take the child out, administer discipline and bring him or her back in. We don't mind if they have to do it fifteen times in one meeting. Within two weeks there are no more problems with the child."

I saw something important in what this pastor's wife was saying. If little Jason becomes noisy and we take him to the nursery, then he is getting what he wants. He can play with toys and do his own thing there. If we take our child to the nursery because of his conduct, then his will is winning over ours! He should be corrected and brought back into the church meeting.

It is also worth noting that when the chief

priests and scribes saw the children crying out to Jesus, "Hosanna to the Son of David!," they were upset and complained to Him. Jesus replied, "Have you never read, 'Out of the mouths of babes and nursing infants You have perfected praise'?" (Matt. 21:16, NKJV). It appears to me these must have been very young children rather than seven- to ten-year-olds, otherwise the statement made by Jesus would not have been correct.

Most churches provide children's activities such as crafts, painting, drawing, coloring, etc. They realize that we cannot just teach the children. We must also do something practical to keep them interested. We agree in principle. But we think you can keep the children's interest by teaching them how to move in the gifts of the Spirit and by taking them out to share the gospel and learn to be bold soul-winners. This will provide all the excitement and adventure they need!

Young People Need Adventure

Many teenagers are bored today. They are looking for thrills, excitement, adventure and daring things to do. They often think their parents live dull, routine, mediocre lives, and they do not want to follow the same pattern.

This is one reason why many of them turn to sin. Drugs, illicit sex, wild parties and petty crime offer them thrills and excitement. A unique kind of daring rises up within them. They often dare each other to do this or that until it becomes sinful or dangerous. Rebelling against authority can be a particularly thrilling challenge for teens.

Christian youngsters find it hard to resist the

rebellion among their peers at school and college. Christianity is regarded by their friends as wimpy and restricting. I saw this firsthand when I was preaching in a church in Tennessee recently. After the first meeting a couple of girls made an interesting comment to their mother when I mentioned witnessing at school. "Mom, talking about Jesus at school is socially unacceptable," they said.

In other words, they were frightened about being ridiculed or becoming unpopular. What they did not realize is that Christianity is not wimpy. Christian author Winkie Pratney once displayed a bumper sticker which read: "Hell Is for Wimps," he said at a meeting in Gainesville, Florida. Christian young people need to learn to accept the persecution that comes with their calling. "All that will live godly in Christ Jesus shall suffer persecution" (2 Tim. 3:12).

Any fool can serve sin and the devil, but it takes courage to stand for Christ in the midst of a crowd of unbelievers. Pratney commented to me once over lunch: "Children are still looking for excitement and the supernatural. That's why they flock to see horror movies about demons and monsters. But the ultimate horror movie is yet to be made — the only trouble is the filmmakers can't make it. It's about the judgment of God. Even the demons tremble at the thought of that!"

We are supposed to have the supernatural happening in our meetings and lives. When it comes to daring this or that, our youngsters need to dare to believe God and act on it. When our kids are totally committed to go all the way with God and be led by the Spirit, they will experience all the thrills and adventure they can handle. It's no use to give the average teenager just enough religion to make him miserable; he should experience God's power and the abundant life that Jesus came to give (John 10:10).

Preaching to Small Children

Some people believe that you cannot preach deep truths to small children because they will not understand. They suggest that you must tell them a little and then some more later, but I disagree. I always preach "the whole counsel of God" to them, regardless of age (Acts 20:27, NKJV). I preach about dying to self, taking up the cross, making Jesus absolute Lord and reasons for being bold and courageous for God. I challenge them to be filled with the Holy Spirit and on fire for the Lord!

My business is to preach the whole truth. The Holy Spirit's business is to make them understand. I cannot play God and decide what they can or cannot understand. Charles Spurgeon often mentioned the need to preach the whole counsel of God to children regardless of age (see his book *Come, Ye Children*). He said that the younger they are saved, the better. Don't wait until they are older, because old people who get saved only have a few years left to serve God, he reasoned. But when small children are converted, they have their whole lives for God to use. He came under some criticism by his contemporaries for preaching this, but he firmly believed that ministering to children was an awesome calling.[1]

We have noticed that in many churches small

children are allowed to come into the main service with coloring books and toys. This is supposed to keep them quiet and occupied during the preaching. We have found that this is not a good policy because it encourages the children to ignore the ministry that is taking place. Some people say, "It's all right as long as they're using Bible coloring books." But we believe it is still a mistake.

I remember being invited to preach at a church in Georgia where all the children were asked to stay in the main service. I was just about to preach when I noticed a small boy of about six years of age sitting on the front row busily coloring. He was very quiet and not bothering anyone. I stood on the platform and addressed the youngster through the microphone. "Young man," I said, "what are you doing?"

"I'm coloring," he replied.

"Well, put away your coloring book now. I have come to preach to you," I replied.

He promptly put away the coloring book and crayons, sat down again on the pew and faced the front. I preached for almost an hour, and he did not take his eyes off of me even once. When I gave an invitation, he was the first to come forward for prayer!

We recently took fifteen to twenty children — ranging from six-year-olds to teenagers — onto a university campus to witness to students. Before we went out, I taught them a lesson on Christian apologetics. I was told that young children could not understand such things, but they loved it! They were thrilled to learn about the proofs for the existence of God, the diety of Christ, the evidence of creation, the foolishness of evolution. After we returned from our witnessing endeavor, the children were on cloud nine. They were excited about how God had used them.

After the children had witnessed to one man, he asked me if I had coerced them to talk to people. I said, "No, they coerced me." They had been bugging me for days to take them witnessing!

As previously mentioned, we live in an age characterized by the pursuit of pleasure, and this affects our children more than we realize. It has been our experience that children have an insatiable appetite for pleasure. Whether it be sports, amusements or outings of any type, youngsters want to have fun. Now there may be nothing wrong with this if it is done in moderation, but it is often done in excess.

How many times have you taken your children out for some treat, such as a trip to a theme park or to the beach, only to find that when you return home they are looking for something else to do. You have spent much time and money only to hear them say that they are bored and want a new adventure!

John Wesley and the leaders of the early Methodist movement did not allow their children to indulge in toys or other amusements. They believed that they should teach their children about the brevity of life and the importance of being productive for the kingdom of God.[2] Perhaps they overemphasized their vision, but we must still ask ourselves: Have we allowed the pendulum to swing too far the other way?

You have heard the argument: "They're only young once, so let them have a good time." But we must not fall into the trap of giving our children all the pleasures they desire. The church must not attempt to compete with the world in regard to entertaining children. The world can do it better. Besides, the fun that the world offers is always tainted with the spice and glitter of forbidden fruit. What the church needs today is a radical alternative!

Children and Entertainment

We all know that children love to play. Play can be athletics, games or just running around. The important thing we must remember about playing is that it is make-believe. Even we adults like to play. We watch television, play video games, read stories, go to movies and attend football or baseball games. Nothing is wrong with enjoying games and make-believe, but to many people these games can become real, especially sports. They are supposed to be games, but people get very serious about them.

Sometimes they fight with others over their favorite teams. The players often get very angry with one another as the spirit of competition takes over, and even countries get upset when their teams don't do well in the Olympics or other international competitions. Many people make their living with sports, so they take them very seriously. I was told of a youngster (in a Christian school!) who asked his basketball coach whether he could attend a Benny Hinn crusade but was refused because he was told the basketball matches were first priority. Many people live only for these things because they know nothing of the reality of Christ.

In the area of make-believe, movies and entertainment, music has a leading role. Music also plays a very important role in the lives of Christian adults as well as teenagers. It is very difficult today to get into the controversy with regard to certain aspects of contemporary Christian music. One must realize that there really is no such thing as Christian music, Christian art, Christian drama or Christian business. To do so would be to commercialize the gospel, and it would no longer be the gospel.

As Christians, our music, art, business and so forth should certainly be *influenced* by our Christian convictions and our understanding of the Scriptures. Probably all music that has been used by the church down through the ages has been the popular music of that particular era. Some of the music of the great composers of history was later used by Christian hymn writers and adopted by churches. What we now call gospel music was country music of the last generation. The popular music for today's young Christians is now called contemporary Christian rock, which is also modeled after secular music.

No matter what the style is called, music, like art, depicts the spiritual climate of the age. When life has no purpose or meaning to many people, it is seen in their music and art. When people get involved in depravity and the occult, it is again seen in their music and art.

Discord, lack of melody and lack of harmony in music are ungodly because God is a God of order, harmony and peace (see Gen. 1:1-3; Eph. 5:18-19 for evidences of God's nature). Therefore, much of what we know as so-called contemporary Christian rock is ungodly regardless of the lyrics. We must evaluate not only the words that are sung, but also the music that is played. Music, like art, has a spirit to it which can be negative or positive (see Phil. 4:8 for the traits of a positive spirit).

Youngsters often ask me about rock or rap music. The spirit behind the music is often the key to my answer. Rap music seems to be mainly associated with a street-wise kid culture. These little guys are dressed in clothes too large for them, shooting obscene words out of the sides of their mouths and calling everybody "man" regardless of their age or sex. They show no respect for their elders and are only willing to learn from their own peers. Can the church adopt that style of music without receiving the spirit behind it?

When society becomes decadent, the art it creates is also tainted. This is why we see rebellion, anger, confusion, disorder and lack of restraint being depicted in the musical style and delivery of modern songs. We must, therefore, be careful about adopting the worldly style of music in our worship and church meetings.

This is not to say that we cannot have good music or that all contemporary Christian music is tainted. Many Christian artists are producing anointed recordings today. We only offer this as a challenge to you to become discerning and watchful about the music your children and teenagers listen to at home.

In the film industry, actors and actresses are paid large sums of money for their work in make-believe. Millions of people pay money to be entertained and brought into the world of make-believe. Places like Disney World have been created, along with Mickey Mouse and similar characters, to help us forget our problems and have fun. We are not denying the value of relaxation, having fun or participating in sports. But doing so must be secondary in our objectives and our children's objectives.

People often ask one another, "What do you do for a pastime?" or "What do you do to kill time?" Christians should never look on this life as just an opportunity to pass time or kill time. We don't have to find something fun to do to stop from being bored. The Bible says that we should be "redeeming the time, because the days are evil" (Eph. 5:16). *Redeem* means to save or not waste something, to buy it back.

Many ungodly people living around us are wasting their lives because they do not know Christ. We must be careful not to allow our children to fall into the same trap or the same habits. We cannot let them spend all their time "goofing off," we must find ways to inspire them to work for God.

The most exciting thing that children can do is work for God — to serve Him and to be the soldiers that He is calling them to be. They always need to be looking for opportunities to inspire others — children and adults — with the message of salvation. Jesus said it is far better to give than to receive, and that is so true. If our children live selfish lives, just wanting to please themselves, they will never be truly happy and never know the blessings of God.

Remember this: Because children love to play and make-believe, it is very possible for them to play at being a Christian. Christianity is not make-believe, however. Jesus is not like Mickey Mouse or Superman. He is real, and one day He will judge the whole world. Many children — especially teenagers — pretend to be Christians and pretend to love the Lord. They think that they can play the Christian game and maybe get serious about God when they are older. It is very dangerous for them to think and believe this way.

Before the first followers of Christ were ever called "Christians," they were known as *disciples* (Acts 11:26). A disciple is one who is being trained and disciplined, one who is in God's boot camp. They are committed, serious soldiers who are in training for the Lord. When youngsters have proven their discipleship, then they have earned the right to be called "Christians." The New Testament certainly does not teach that you become a Christian first, and then sometime down the road you have the option of becoming a disciple.

Let's not allow our children to make their age an excuse to fool around with God. He will not accept this. Let's all be willing to be trained in God's boot camp, even if it is strenuous. If we don't give up, but persevere to the end, we will see results. Remember: Always ask the Holy Spirit to fill you and to give you His power to make this possible. If you ask believing, He will.

CHAPTER TWO

WHAT DOES GOD EXPECT FROM CHILDREN?

H ow can we know what God expects from children? To answer this question we will first study the Scriptures to see how God used certain children in ministry. There are also amazing, though little known, accounts of children's roles in revivals of the eighteenth, nineteenth and twentieth centuries, and we will provide some examples. Finally, my wife and I are continually privileged to be eyewitnesses of God's willingness to use children, and we will share some of our personal experiences in children's ministry.

In 1 Samuel 1 we read the story of Hannah, who was desperate to have a child. She prayed to God and vowed that if He would bless her with a son, she would dedicate him to the service of the Lord. She did not just take him to a dedication service but literally gave him over to be trained by the man of God.

God answered Hannah's prayer of faith and she gave birth to a son whom she named Samuel. He had a great destiny — he would become a prophet of God. When she brought him to the temple, he was probably between two and three years of age, yet we read that Samuel "worshipped the Lord there" (v. 28). He also ministered unto the Lord and before the Lord (1 Sam. 2:11,18). Notice that the Bible does not say he was learning to minister. He was actually doing the ministering at that young age!

Another great example of how God wants to use children can be found in the life of Moses. He was only three months old when his mother hid him in a basket in the Nile River. Pharoah's daughter found him and arranged for his mother to nurse the baby for the first few years of his life until he was weaned (Ex. 2:1-10). All the training in the first few years of his life was to determine his destiny! But his mother and father were people of faith, for we are told in Hebrews 11:23:

> By faith Moses, when he was born, was hid three months of his parents, because they saw he was a proper child; and they were not afraid of the king's commandment.

His parents imparted that same faith to their son during the first few years of his life. In Hebrews 11:24 we read:

> By faith Moses, when he was come to

> years, refused to be called the son of
> Pharoah's daughter; choosing rather to
> suffer affliction with the people of God,
> than to enjoy the pleasure of sin for a
> season.

Where did Moses learn this faith? Certainly not in Pharoah's house or in the classrooms of Egypt!

This one example should convince us that Christian parents can make a deep impression upon their young infants by training them in the ways of righteousness! We do not have to wait until our children are old enough to read, write or even walk! Tiny children can experience the love of God and the power of His Spirit.

God did not leave out the teenagers in Bible days, either. In the Old Testament we read of the account of Joseph and how God gave him a dream when he was a seventeen-year-old (Gen. 37). We also read of Samuel hearing the voice of God when he had barely reached his teens. He received a message of judgment for the high priest, his sons and the nation of Israel that he was scared to even talk about!

We also read about David, who — although he was only a youth — was able to slay the giant Goliath (1 Sam. 17). Most Bible scholars believe that Mary was just a teenager when the angel Gabriel visited her and announced that she had been specially chosen by God to be the mother of Jesus (Luke 1:26-38).

Jesus' Example

In the New Testament we read how Jesus confounded the Jewish teachers in the temple when he was only twelve years old. In Luke 2:40-41 we read of Him: "And the child grew, and waxed strong in spirit, filled with wisdom: and the grace of God was upon him." When His parents questioned him after they had been separated in Jerusalem, Jesus responded, "Did you not know that I must be about My Father's business?" (Luke 2:49, NKJV).

Would to God that the average twelve-year-old American Christian child would have the same attitude! By the age of twelve Jesus had developed the maturity of an adult. He was able to think, reason and discuss matters of theology and morality with strong conviction — so much so that the wise religious leaders of the day were confounded.

This was not simply because Jesus was the Son of God. He was not performing as a super-child or exercising extraordinary divine powers. Jesus had been trained diligently in the Word of God by His parents and other teachers, and He had been nurtured in the faith of Israel. He had also been filled with God's wisdom and grace by the Holy Spirit. We should indeed expect our children today to possess the same faith, the same anointing and the same knowledge of God's Word.

In Luke 1:15 we read that John the Baptist was filled with the Holy Ghost from his mother's womb, yet Jesus said in Luke 7:28 that the least in the kingdom of God was greater than John the Baptist. What are we believing for our children?

In Paul's second letter to his beloved disciple Timothy, he wrote, "From a child thou hast known the holy scriptures, which are able to make thee wise unto salvation through faith which is in Christ Jesus" (2 Tim. 3:15). Paul mentions the faith which was in Timothy's grandmother, mother and in him also (2 Tim. 1:5). Are we cultivating this faith in our children today? Are we hiding the precious truths of the holy Scriptures in their tender hearts? Jeremiah said that he was but a child, but God still called him to be a prophet to the nation (Jer. 1:4-8).

Modern Examples

God did not stop using children after the New Testament was written, either. If we do a study of church history and of past revivals, we will find that God used youngsters many times in mighty ways.

In fact, many people say that 80 percent of all missionaries received their call to the mission field when they were children. This should indicate to us that God is still in the business of calling children, just as he called Samuel while he was yet a young boy.

Jonathan Edwards, one of the greatest theologians America ever produced, entered Yale University when he was thirteen and graduated as valedictorian at age seventeen.

Catherine Booth, the wife of William Booth, founder of the Salvation Army, reportedly read the Bible through many times before the age of twelve. Frances Ridley Havergal (1836-1879) is known for writing a number of hymns. Her father was a minister with the Church of England. Several sources have reported that she knew the New Testament and the book of Psalms by heart by the age of three. By the time she was five years old she could read it in the Greek.

Some people might find that hard to believe or think that this child was just one of those special geniuses who pop up every so often in history. This is not so. A popular book on child development cites numerous accounts of children as young as twenty months old who are able to read five thousand words; play violins; and do math, algebra and geometry.[1]

These are all ordinary children who have had training that unlocked their natural abilities. While I am not advocating these kinds of programs, they illustrate that we sometimes underestimate our children's abilities. This is why I am opposed to nursery and only play-type ministry in the church. We must not waste our children's spiritual and mental potential.

The famous Welsh revival at the turn of this century was led by twenty-one-year-old Evan Roberts. Many of Roberts's friends were young men barely out of their teens. During that move of the Holy Spirit, young children often went out into the streets singing and witnessing. Large meetings grew out of their testimony.[2]

In 1970 a powerful revival broke out among students in their teens and early twenties at Asbury College in Wilmore, Kentucky. The move started during the regular 10 A.M. chapel service, and students remained in prayer in the auditorium until 10:30 that night. Lectures were cancelled for several days as students prayed, sang and gave testimonies.[3]

A teenager also played a key role during a revival in the Hebrides (a group of islands off the coast of Scotland), which occurred between 1949 and 1952. A seventeen-year-old boy named Donald Smith was given an amazing ministry of prayer. In the town of Berneray, religious life was at a low ebb. A message was sent to the praying men of Barvas to send for the young Donald. Halfway through the message, the preacher called out, "Donald, will you lead us in prayer?" Standing to his feet, he began to pour out his heart before God in agonizing intercession for the people of the island, reminding God that he was the great "covenant-keeping God."

> Suddenly it seemed as though the heavens were rent and God swept into the church. People everywhere were stricken by the power of God as the Spirit swept through in great convicting power. Outside, startling things were taking place. Simultaneously the Spirit of God had swept over the homes and the area around the village, and everywhere people were coming under great conviction of sin.
>
> By ten o'clock the roads were black with people streaming to the church from every direction. People gripped each other in fear. In agony of soul they trembled; many wept and some fell to the ground in great conviction of sin.[4]

A book titled *Accounts of Religious Revivals in Many Parts of the United States* has some interesting stories about this move among the Baptist communities. One fifteen-year-old girl came under conviction for several weeks. She was constantly crying out, "Mercy! Mercy!" and finally lost the power of speech. She sat trembling for about an hour and then finally burst forth into raptures of joy and praise after having found salvation. Her tongue was liberated, and she began to speak unknown strains. This particular revival affected people from age nine to eighty.[5]

A revival in the Congo in 1934 also resulted in children who were convicted by the power of the Holy Spirit. In one case small toddlers confessed to stealing food that their mothers hid away for the evening meal. With tears streaming down their faces, they told their mothers that they had lied when they denied taking the food. School girls confessed to running off from school to go to dances secretly. School boys owned up to stealing animals out of other boys' traps.[6]

School children were evangelizing adults during the revival in Wales in 1904. In the day schools the children would pray and sing with great effect as the Spirit moved on them. One day a four-year-old put up his hand to get the teacher's attention. "What is it?" asked the teacher. "Please, teacher. Do you love Jesus?" the boy asked. The response to that question was that the teacher was saved then and there and eventually became a missionary to India.[7]

It was also common for children to take the initiative and show spiritual concern for their parents during the Nova Scotia revival of 1782. Women and children had a key role in bringing about various local revivals, according to the book *Ravished by the Spirit* by G.A. Rawlyk.[8]

Young people were especially active in a revival

in Liverpool, Nova Scotia, in 1807. Small boys and girls witnessed during the day and had meetings at night. The adults complained that their meetings were too noisy because of the constant yelling. They wanted order and sermons, but the children refused to let the Holy Spirit be quenched. Rawlyk's book also says that women, children and young people affected the vast majority of people during the Second Great Awakening in New England in the 1790s.[9]

An account of the early beginnings of the Salvation Army stated that the expansion and early success of the movement was only possible through its officers, most of them young women.[10]

Children have always been open to the supernatural realm. The Roman Catholic Church has had many revered saints who were either children or teenagers, including Joan of Arc, St. Thérèsa of Lisieux and St. Bernadette. While some of these children's experiences may not have had divine origins, their lives still demonstrate that children are sensitive to the things of the spirit realm.

Fifteen-year-old Sammy Morris, known as the Ebony Saint, came to the United States from Africa at the beginning of this century. His journey to America was initiated after he came out of the African jungle and stumbled upon a Christian settlement. There he learned to read and write and was converted to Christianity.

Sammy developed a tremendous hunger for the Holy Spirit. He had met a Spirit-filled woman who had told him that she had learned about the Holy Spirit from a man named Stephen Merritt, who lived in the United States. "I will go and see this man," said Sammy, and he went rushing off to the docks to find a ship. He had no money for his passage but just trusted his heavenly Father to provide. He ended up working for his passage as a cabin boy.

The captain of the ship was a rough, foul-mouthed drunkard, and most of the crew were violent men, especially a large Malaysian who hated all Negroes and planned to kill Sammy. Initially Sammy experienced much physical abuse because the whole crew resented his presence. Yet he quietly prayed for the officers and crew. He then found some who were sick and prayed for them. They were healed instantly. He then prayed openly for them all and sang worship songs to them during the long voyage.

During his time on the ship Sammy's anointing was so felt that most of the men's attitudes were turned around. Sammy and the Malaysian became close friends, especially after Sammy prayed for him when he was very sick and an instant healing took place.

When Sammy disembarked in New York, many of the hardened crew wept. As he got off the ship, he called out to a stranger and asked where he could find Stephen Merritt. The stranger said he had been at the Bethel Mission, which was run by Merritt, and he would take him there.

When Sammy arrived at the mission, Merritt was just leaving for a meeting. Sammy told him he had just come from Africa and he wanted to learn about the Holy Spirit. Merritt, somewhat amused by this, said if he would wait in the mission, he would return to talk to him later. When Merritt returned to the mission, he found seventeen men prostrate on their faces before Sammy as he told them about Jesus. Needless to say, Merritt wondered what was left for him to teach the young lad about the Holy Spirit!

This precious young saint died before he was twenty-one years old, but God used him mightily during those short years.[11]

In the early part of this century God moved in a powerful way among very small street children who were being taught to read and write in a mission school in China. They were taken up into heaven, walked the streets of the heavenly Jerusalem, met with angels and were completely transformed from heathen sinners into saints. This unusual revival, recorded now in the book *Visions Beyond the Veil*, lasted many weeks and had a profound impact on all those around that area at the time.[12]

A man of God whom we have known for about twenty years told us a story about his experiences pastoring a church in the north of England in 1932. In the service there was a group of teenage girls who used to giggle and chew gum while he was preaching. The ringleader of the group was a girl named Lizzie.

After a while the pastor was transferred to another work. One day he was in a meeting with a group of Pentecostal ministers, and they were discussing a rumor about a revival which had broken out in a church. He soon discovered they were talking about the church he used to pastor. He thought, "That couldn't be so! If any true revival had happened, I would have been there." They discussed the pros and cons of the situation and decided to send him back to investigate.

He arrived at the church to find the place packed with people. To his dismay he saw Lizzie walking about with her hands outstretched and her eyes tightly closed as she prophesied over people and gave them words of knowledge. Many were also being slain in the Spirit!

"This is not God," the pastor said to himself. "She's peeking. And, besides, God would definitely not use her." He stood in the back, and she slowly advanced toward him. So he made his way around to the other end of the church. She stopped in the middle with her eyes still closed, turned and walked toward him.

"If she touches me, I'll spit in her face," the pastor thought. She finally came right up, laid her hands on him and told him all that he had been thinking. He said that the power of the Holy Spirit went through his body, and he collapsed in a heap, weeping. God had used a formerly rebellious teenager to deal with his pride. He said that the revival lasted for two years and affected a number of churches in the town. They had meetings every night which never finished before two o'clock in the morning.

In our own ministry we have also witnessed God using children in miraculous ways. A short while ago a nine-year-old girl was lying on the floor under the power of the Holy Spirit in one of our meetings. She obviously could not get up. My wife asked her about her problem, and the little girl responded that a few weeks earlier she had said to her mother, "I don't believe your God is real."

However, her attitude changed after her encounter with God that night. "Now I know He is real," she told us, "because He is stronger than me." After she made this statement, she was able to get up but had extreme difficulty walking. Her legs just didn't seem to want to move. At that point, recognizing what God was trying to teach her, I said to the girl, "You need to walk in the Lord's way."

"That's another thing I said to my mother, 'I don't want to walk this way.' But I will! I will!" she exclaimed, and immediately she was released to walk normally.

I distinctly remember the first meeting I conducted with the children at a Kenneth Copeland Believer's Convention in Brighton, England. The woman in charge of the children's ministry had arranged for me to be the guest speaker. She was an actress by profession, and her husband was a musician. They had organized five full days of meetings, complete with puppet shows, stage props and drama presentations for about 350 children. After I ministered the first night, she came to me rather discouraged and said, "It's not fair! I spent hundreds of dollars on all these props and a great deal of time rehearsing the skits, and you walk in with just a Bible, preach to the children and the Holy Spirit falls immediately. Then you leave and we are left to pick up the pieces. I want to learn what you are doing so I don't have to trust in my props any longer!"

Very soon she and her husband were ministering with me during the remainder of the meetings, and the power of God moved in a mighty way.

Although she continued to use her props from time to time, much of the ensuing ministry was not entertaining the children but equipping them in how they could be effective in God's army. Many of the adults came down from the main service and attended, saying that the children's meetings were as good as the adult service! The children were laying hands on their parents, praying for them and seeing them healed, delivered and slain under the power of the Spirit.

Someone then jumped onto the platform where Copeland was ministering and reported how the Spirit was moving in the children's meetings. At that point Copeland prophesied to the congregation that the next revival would come through children!

A number of years ago we were ministering at a family camp in Ohio. We were given responsibility for the teenagers. Another minister was speaking to the children, and another was ministering to the adults. We found that many of the teenagers were not interested in spiritual things and were resisting the Holy Spirit. Although we had made some progress with them after two days, it was still an uphill battle.

We decided to ask if we could minister to the younger children the next afternoon. We had a group of about thirty children between the ages of five and ten. I shared the salvation message with them, prayed for some who wanted to surrender to Christ and prayed for the remainder of them to receive the baptism of the Holy Spirit. Then we simply sat down and waited.

After a period of time some of them began to weep and confess their sins. Some fell down under the power of the Spirit, and a six-year-old boy had a very detailed prophetic vision of America.

When we were finally finished, we asked the youngsters to walk up the hill to the main building where the adults were staying. Halfway up the hill, the children caught up with the teenagers, and the Holy Spirit began to move upon them as well! This resulted in their falling down on the ground with tears of repentance. We were already in the sanctuary because we had driven our car, and we were listening to the musicians arranging songs for the meeting that evening. The guest minister was also there preparing his evening message.

Suddenly the doors burst open, and the children and teenagers came pouring in. As soon as they did, the Holy Spirit fell on the adults! People began to laugh, weep and get healed and delivered. Some danced, while others shouted and praised. Needless to say, the musicians were not able to sing their prepared songs that night, and the guest speaker never delivered his message! This revival lasted for two days!

On another occasion we were at a family retreat on a small island off the coast of England. We had finished the evening meeting at a Christian hotel and were in the reception area having some refreshments before bedtime. Some of the teenagers, however, had asked to stay in the meeting room to pray.

Suddenly we heard some screaming and shouting, and someone ran over to us from the meeting room and asked us to come quickly. When we entered the room, we saw a sixteen-year-old Catholic boy (who had been saved that weekend) kneeling in the middle of the room. He was in a trance, and his right arm and hand were outstretched while his finger pointed like the hand of a clock as he revolved slowly in the center of the room.

As his finger pointed to someone, they would fall under the power of the Holy Spirit. We recognized that it was the finger of God setting people free. After a while we returned to our room to finish our refreshments, and then suddenly the presence of God came again! People slowly put their drinks down and began to weep; others fell under the power of God.

A short while after this lifted, we suddenly heard the noise of screaming and shouting from upstairs where the children were sleeping. All of the small children ran downstairs; the Holy Spirit had been visiting them as well! God had done the same thing at that retreat as He had done at the family camp in Ohio, only in a different sequence.

Recently we have seen small children praying for adults, even ministers, and we have watched the power of God move through them. When our eleven-year-old daughter prayed for a church secretary, the young lady came under the anointing of the Holy Spirit and was laid out on the floor for more than four hours as God spoke many things to her about her past. As the Holy Spirit moves, our youngest daughter, Lisa, is often able to tell adults the potential ministry they have or confirm their callings and gifts. In our meetings we have seen young children repenting, weeping and laughing as the Holy Spirit has become real to them. Many of them have fallen under the power of God, and some have even remained transfixed for lengthy periods of time.

We were once preaching in a church in Ohio.

The children were down in the basement while we were ministering to the adults. At the end of the message we started to minister in the Holy Spirit. Suddenly the children came up from the basement, and the Spirit fell on them. One very small child of about four years of age was transfixed in the Spirit for forty minutes with her hands in the air. She then fell to her knees and stayed there with her hands in the air for another ten minutes. I remember the pastor walking around her in amazement, saying to various people, "Look at that! Have you ever seen anything like it?"

In one large meeting in Illinois a little boy of about six suddenly lost his ability to talk. He was pointing to his mouth with an alarmed look on his face and making strange noises. A group of youngsters were gathered around, saying, "He can't talk; he can't talk." I prayed for him, but nothing happened. I asked him if he had been saying foolish things that were not honoring to the Lord. He nodded his head. I told him to repent. He bowed his head and repented. I prayed for him again, and his voice immediately came back. He went off happily with the other children.

This chapter was titled with a question: What does God expect from children? Our experiences have all been evidence of a simple truth: God expects them to be useful in the kingdom. He *wants* to use them! He wants to reveal Himself to them and move through them. We must forever reject the idea that children should sit on the sidelines while God is at work.

CHAPTER THREE

EQUIPPING GOD'S YOUNG ARMY FOR MINISTRY

The greatest need in the church today is for young children and teenagers to be equipped for the work of the ministry. The task of "equipping the saints for the work of service" must include children (Eph. 4:11-12, NAS). God desires to send His apostles, prophets, evangelists, pastors and teachers to the youth. I believe that He is indeed raising up these ministries today in order to reach a great army of youngsters. These ministers will not be dressed up as cowboys, pirates, clowns or Disney characters. They will be seen as generals and commanders in God's army.

> This charge I commit unto thee...that thou...mightest war a good warfare (1 Tim. 1:18).

Let's begin our explanation of the five-fold ministry of the church by looking at the *apostles* to the youth. Today we need apostles who can inspire and train young men and women, raise up anointed pastors and evangelists, and release armies of youngsters in many churches to preach the gospel and demonstrate a life-style that is different from the world's. We need these children's leaders to show the church that they should take God's call on children seriously, and we need them to show youth, children and Sunday school workers the need for a radical change in children's ministry.

We need *prophets* to the youth to work with the apostles, increasing the vision of a mighty army of children that God desires to bring forth in this generation. These prophets need to bring the spirit of prophecy to the children, giving them a sense of divine destiny and revealing His specific will for their lives. These prophets must encourage the flow of the Holy Spirit's gifts in children's meetings and maintain a prophetic vision of the future in the hearts of our young people (Prov. 29:18; Joel 2:28; Acts 2:17).

We need youth *pastors* who realize that they have been set apart for the ministry and called of God (Rom. 1:1). Their number-one priority should be to have God's anointing and approval on their lives and ministry. If they are to raise up an army, then they must understand their position of authority.

Military officers do not usually fraternize with the privates in the army; otherwise they lose their authority and respect. Youth leaders are expected to be the anointed leaders and inspirers of the youngsters. They are not to be involved in children's recreational activities or simply fulfill the role of a children's activities director.

Many churches employ a youth pastor to be nothing more than an errand boy for a thousand different church needs, as well as a recreational director for the children's play time. This is a shame. It is imperative that youth pastors dedicate themselves to the spiritual needs of the youngsters and have the church hire someone else to organize recreational activities.

Many youth pastors and workers become involved in youth work simply because they enjoy being with children or because they enjoy doing the things that children like to do. In fact, they are often just big kids themselves! This does not line up with God's standard: There is a price to pay for ministry. Although we are expected to show love and friendliness to every member of the body of Christ (Rom. 12:10; 2 Pet. 1:7), there is a certain loneliness for the person who has been "set apart for the ministry."

A couple of years ago I was ministering to the children's pastors at a Vineyard church in Denver, Colorado. This remarkable church has 350 children's pastors that minister to 2,700 children under the direction of Lenny LaGuardia. Lenny showed me a seven-year-old boy. "He tried to kill his mother recently," he said. "You can't take kids like him, sit them in Sunday school and tell them Bible stories. These kids come from abusive, dysfunctional, single-parent homes, and they need true pastoral care." We need to train people to be real pastors to the youngsters.

I was once in a large church in North Carolina

where I was asked to minister to the youth on a Sunday evening. When I arrived, the youth pastor said, "We don't usually have any preaching on Sunday evenings. We just eat pizza and then play games. After we have eaten our pizza, you are welcome to minister. I don't know where these kids are spiritually, but they are a good bunch of kids."

I did not organize games for them. I preached. Some got angry with me, and some started to cry. The youth pastor went pale and said that he almost came forward himself when I made the call for repentance. This youth pastor was missing the mark. He was more interested in pleasing the young people than in pleasing the Lord.

In the past I have seen problems with the children some people call "preachers' kids." Many adults in full-time ministry have been so busy with the church and the Lord's work that they have neglected their children. Their kids have either grown up hating their parents or hating Christianity.

In recent years there has been much ministry to pastors in this situation. The major focus is an attempt to put balance in their lives. Pastors have been told that their families are more important than the work of the Lord and that they need to put them first. Many have found themselves in a dilemma and do not know quite what to do.

We believe the answer is simple. Obviously our wives and children are a part of the Lord's work and are our first disciples. Yet we cannot neglect the church. Neither can we neglect our families. The solution is to have our children be an extension of our ministry and let them become a very important part of our vision.

If Kathie and I were just to go off and minister to other people and leave our children to themselves, then that would be the thin end of the wedge. No! They are involved in what we do, and they are learning to see that their future is already being mapped out by God in service for Him. They spend more time with us than most children do, and we not only play together but work together. (That is not to say that our children do not enjoy playing with other children during free times or when we return from long trips.)

I have noticed that adults who are interested in reaching rebellious young people in the church will often try to befriend them by playing games and doing fun things with them. The kids often complain that they are tired of being preached at and that no one cares for their needs. So these misguided people bend over backward trying to please the kids so as to avoid turning them off.

But think about it. If these youngsters did not want to live selfish lives and just do their own thing, they wouldn't mind being preached to and would be happy to respond in a positive way to the Word of God. I have yet to understand what is wrong with being preached at. I have always believed that preaching is one of the most important and scriptural ways of reaching people for the Lord.

Many years ago in England, local churches used to have youth clubs. These were places where youngsters could come and listen to records, play table tennis and billiards, have refreshments and meet each other. The motive behind the clubs was to reach youngsters with the gospel. About five minutes before the end of the evening the pastor would appear and give a little spiritual talk, a mini-sermonette. The result of these endeavors was usually zero. The youngsters didn't mind putting up with five minutes of "spiritual claptrap" in exchange for two hours of free food and facilities.

The gospel is never effective when it is tagged on to the end of something else and not given first place.

Youth pastors, because they are shepherds, need to have genuine love and compassion for the youngsters, of course. In fact, they must love them so much that they will give them what they need — not what they want. They cannot be concerned about being popular with the youngsters. They must be willing to be misunderstood when they endeavor to protect the youth from themselves. When the youth see that their pastors are sincere and willing to lay down their lives for them because they desire God's best for their lives, there will be wonderful results.

Learning the Ways of the Spirit

Many pastors do not understand the ways of the Spirit in preaching to children. Before we begin to communicate the Word of God to children, we must realize that there is a spiritual battle going on. The majority of untrained children in the church bring the spirit of the world into meetings. This may be done unconsciously, but that makes no difference. It can still make the preaching of little effect.

What is this spirit of the world? Perhaps a better term would be the spirit of unreality, which affects so many youth meetings. It is a general attitude that we are gathering only to goof off, and it is coupled with a lack of seriousness about the things of God. If this spirit is not broken in meetings, it will rule, and the youth worker or Sunday school teacher will be controlled by it as well.

Youth leaders may think they have authority in such a setting, but at best it will only be an ecclesiastical authority and not a spiritual one. The situation reminds me of the story of the small boy who would not sit down.

"Sit down!" said one adult in charge.

"I won't sit down," replied the small boy.

"Sit down or I'll knock you down," exclaimed the adult angrily.

The little boy sat down and said defiantly, "But I'm still standing up inside."

The adult had authority, but it was not true spiritual authority.

The youth pastor or teacher must be prepared for spiritual battle. They must pray and prepare themselves for the meeting (Eph. 6:18) so that the anointing of God rests on them. The anointing will break the power of the spirit of the world in the first few seconds of a meeting (1 John 4:4). This is very important. A youth pastor cannot expect to have a spiritual time with the youngsters if he has been goofing off with them before the meeting. Ecclesiastes 3:1-8 tells us that there is a time and place for everything.

I remember being taken to a juvenile detention center by a Christian brother a few years ago. He used to go there for a Tuesday evening "rap" session. The idea was that I would go with him the first Tuesday and see how it went. The following Tuesday I would minister. About fifteen juveniles were present, and they fired questions at him for about an hour on topics ranging from sex and drugs to speaking in tongues and demons. He seemed to be very pleased with the meeting, but I felt that the kids were in control. They seemed to be "jerking him around" with a bombardment of questions and keeping him on the defensive. "Next week you can take them," he said.

"Fine," I said, "but we will *not* have a rap session. I will preach to them."

We arrived the following Tuesday, and he introduced me. (They had seen me the previous week, but during that time I had not said a word.) I preached, and they were visibly shaken. Many were crying and saying, "I thought I was a Christian. Now I'm not so sure." We prayed for many of them, and they asked me if I was going to come again the next week. My friend said, "Yes, he will."

The following week about fifty kids were present. Although we officially had only one hour, we stayed for two hours praying and counseling with the youngsters. Even when we had gone outside, they were calling to us through the grills of their cells and asking for prayer.

Paul said that he was not ashamed of the gospel of Christ because it is the power of God unto salvation (Rom. 1:16). Spiritual authority is essential.

Once we were having a house meeting, and a couple's baby would not stop screaming. Finally we said to the baby, "We command you to be quiet in the name of Jesus." The baby stopped crying immediately, smiled and went to sleep. Spiritual authority is essential.

Many years ago in England we went to preach at a secular school. As we were making our way to the classroom for the meeting, we saw two teenage girls standing outside the principal's office. "Come and join us. We are having a meeting," we said. When the girls saw the guitars, they followed us. When the teacher saw the girls come in, she was very upset.

"Those girls are the worst girls in the school and they are on detention," she said. "They will wreck the meeting."

"We don't believe that," we replied.

At the end of the meeting they were the first to come forward for salvation. Spiritual authority is essential.

In many of the secular schools that we visited, youngsters would try to heckle us, but it would never work. God would give us words of knowledge about the would-be hecklers. Spiritual authority is essential.

I was preaching in a private boarding college in England. We were there for several days. On the last day the ringleader of a group of antagonists put up his hand and expressed his desire to ask a question. Then, in a rather pompous way — and with a number of other boys egging him on — he began to claim that this "Christianity stuff" was for the birds.

He said, "It was OK for ignorant, stupid people

long ago, but in our day of enlightenment we do not need these crutches, this pie in the sky. Man is now sophisticated enough to work out his own problems without having to call on some divine intervention."

His supporters clapped and cheered as he sat down.

"How old are you?" I asked.

"Sixteen," he replied.

"Then you have put me in a difficult situation," I said. I saw him beginning to smirk, and I continued. "Two thousand years ago a man called Jesus Christ made a remarkable impact on history. Millions of people down through the ages have been profoundly affected by Him and His teachings. Apart from His miracles and the miracles which still happen today through His name, His teachings are more profound than the theories of the most learned philosophers. Now I am not a betting man, but if I had to stake my life on whom I would choose to follow — a sixteen-year-old boy or Jesus Christ — I would go for Christ every time."

Spiritual authority is essential.

It is of paramount importance that our youngsters be exposed to anointed preaching and teaching. A pastor would never dream of asking the church if there were any volunteers to preach the sermon on Sunday morning. Yet this is what is often done in the children's church. It is not enough for those in children's ministry to be mature, willing, doctrinally sound and to love children. They must have a divine calling and anointing to do this work (1 Pet. 4:11; 1 Cor. 2:4).

The church must never let children's ministry lapse into a glorified babysitting service that simply keeps children occupied while the adults meet together. Our children must hear the anointed Word preached just like everyone else! Furthermore, in ministry to adults we do not use fantasy to teach Bible truths. Similarly, in teaching children it's dangerous to mix too much fantasy with Bible truths.

Much teaching today focuses on teenage problems such as identity crises, peer pressure, the "rebellious stage," drug and alcohol abuse, promiscuity, teen abortion and pregnancy, suicide and so on. These problems should not be happening among children who are filled with the power of the Holy Spirit! They will happen, however, to lukewarm, carnal believers (Rev. 3:15-16).

Teaching Children: First Things First

Every boy and girl needs to have a real encounter with the Holy Spirit and the person of Christ as Savior and Lord. Do not take their salvation for granted just because they have been raised in a church and have made a profession of faith. Find out how real their conversion is. Children have a way of saying things to keep adults off their backs. They will often profess that they are born again to keep their pastor, youth leaders and parents happy. In addition, if the level of Christianity is poor in the church, home or youth group, children will often gravitate to the lowest level.

Many young people hold to a philosophy that they can have salvation and still do what they please, believing that they can mix the things of God and the things of the world. Many are affected by what goes on around them rather than by what the Bible says.

Meanwhile, many parents of Christian kids live hypocritical lives, living out one behavior pattern at home and another at church. This affects children in a very negative way. Parents must realize they have a very important role to play in their children's Christian experience. They must encourage and show a real interest and involvement in seeing their children trained in God's army. Training, not entertaining — this should be our motto in every children's church and youth group (Acts 1:8; Matt. 16:24-25).

Once a child is exposed to the power of the Holy Spirit and makes a true commitment, then he or she is ready to be trained for God's army. When a child joins the armed forces, he gives up his rights as a civilian. He can no longer do as he pleases. AWOL (absent without leave) is a serious offense. Boot camp trains the child to be disciplined, fit, efficient in warfare and obedient to the commander-in-chief without question. Unlike the human military, the motivation is not force or money but a burning love for Christ and His kingdom.

It is not enough to teach children merely to be good and to obey God's commandments. The purpose of being a Christian is not just to refrain from the things that worldly people do. Many youth groups today lack excitement about being a Christian, and that is why the youngsters turn to other things. Religion will always be boring, but the true Christ-life never is. Salvation is more than being saved from hell and more than being filled with the Holy Spirit. It is being conformed to the image of God's Son and bringing many sons to glory (Rom. 8:29-30; Heb. 2:10).

Children today need to see that they have been called to be soldiers (2 Tim. 2:3-4). Paul told young Timothy:

> Thou therefore enjoy hardness, as a good soldier of Jesus Christ. No man that warreth entangleth himself with the affairs of this life, that he may please him who hath chosen him to be a soldier (2 Tim. 2:4-5).

Children respond positively to the idea of wearing uniforms, carrying weapons and wearing the spiritual armor described in Ephesians 6:10-18. But if they desire to be a part of God's army, then they must subject themselves to boot camp. They must be trained to do warfare against the devil, their enemy, and learn how to rescue others from his domain (1 Tim. 1:18).

You can reinforce Paul's call to be a soldier by having an army or boot camp theme for your children's classes. The children could even wear uniforms, badges or stripes. You could designate some children to be sergeants and corporals in the army, and they would be responsible to call up other children regularly on the telephone and pray with them or minister to them. These young leaders would have to be the most radical kids in the group, and they must have a real compassion and zeal to see the other children become mighty for God.

I would not recommend that you break up children's groups into grades like a school with a teacher for every grade. I would separate them into only two groups: first through fifth grades and sixth through twelfth grades. This way you can keep better control of the groups and make sure that the vision is being carried out properly. You will also be able to discern whether the teachers are anointed in their ministry. If a teacher is anointed, he or she will have no problem in ministering to varying age groups at the same time. The spiritual maturity of the youngsters should be the criterion rather than their natural age.

You would also need to call a meeting for all the parents. At that meeting you should explain the seriousness and importance of ministry to youth. The parents should understand that this is not a church-run babysitting service. They must be committed to bringing their children to every meeting, which requires sacrifice. Many school and social activities, such as cheerleading, dance classes, athletics and so on, will have to be abandoned.

What to Do With the Recruits

We suggest that you organize outreach meetings approximately every two weeks. Reports would be given on a weekly basis as to the progress that individual children were making in their evangelism and other spiritual disciplines. The children would be taught that when you join the army you are not immediately given a rifle and ammunition and then told to "go for it." You have to be trained to work as a disciplined team. The children also need to understand that their commitment to this army is a lifelong commitment.

You should also plan teaching and training sessions, sharing sessions and special times of prayer. The youngsters would be encouraged to become an active part in the outreach meetings through preaching, giving testimonies, playing instruments, doing interpretive dance and so on. Please note that these meetings are in addition to the main church meetings. During those meetings the youngsters should participate with the adults.

The children need to see themselves as part of God's SWAT team on rescue missions (Jude 23). They must learn that their success will not depend on their own ability but on the Lord and the spiritual armor He has provided (1 Cor. 1:27-29; Eph. 6:10-18). They must also see that they are ambassadors representing Christ and His kingdom (2 Cor. 5:20). When children know that they are called to have a prophetic anointing on their lives, then they will realize they have been called to take dominion on this earth for God's glory — and to drive the devil off the land! They will recognize that they are strangers and pilgrims in this world system (1 Pet. 2:11).

Be sure that the children understand faith. Many who profess to be Christians have little real conviction about their beliefs. The world always says, "Seeing is believing." But Christians of all ages are to declare, "Believing is seeing!"

At the same time, you can lead the children toward the reality of Christ and guide them into real experiences with the Holy Spirit. The key is to make sure the children understand that experiences are not necessarily a constant thing. The children must walk in the truth by faith, not by experiences or feelings (2 Cor. 5:7, 13:5).

Teaching the Children to Witness

Another large part of your program should be directed toward teaching children how to witness. The first step is to direct the children to the Word of God. They must learn Scriptures so that they can grow spiritually. You can explain to them that if the Son of God had to memorize and quote Scriptures to defeat the devil, so must they (Matt. 4:4-10).

Show them that the authority for witnessing depends upon the Word of God, not their personal ideas and philosophies (Eph. 6:17). Then you can explain that their life-styles and their testimonies can help make their witnessing more effective, too.

A radical change in what is acceptable today in children's ministry will help to set them on fire. This includes teaching our youngsters the plan of salvation very thoroughly so they can pass on God's message effectively. They must be able to answer these and other questions:

• How does the blood of Christ wash away our sins? How did Christ's death on the cross save us?

• If God is merciful, will He not forgive anybody who is sorry?

• If God is a God of love, how can He send people to hell?

• What about people of other religions, or good people who don't believe the way I do?

Our children must become confident in their beliefs, knowing that they have God's answer for every situation. This is one example of a simple, logical way to teach the plan of salvation:

1) The fact of sin (Rom. 3:10,23; James 4:17,

2:10).

2) The penalty of sin (Rom. 6:23; Ezek. 18:20; Gen. 2:17).

3) The penalty paid by Christ (Is. 53:5-6; Rom. 8:32; 2 Cor. 5:21).

4) The need to accept Jesus Christ as Savior and Lord (John 3:36, 1:12, 8:12,24; Acts 4:12).

Once the youngsters have a biblical understanding of truth, they are ready to learn to communicate it. Learning to write down the gospel message on an index card is a good class project. This enables youngsters to articulate the gospel message clearly and concisely. You can also have the children practice "fishing for men" through role-playing. Let some play the role of the seeker and the others the role of the witness. This can be done in a group, with each one taking turns while the others critique.

The youngsters need encouragement to keep their conversation on the Person and claims of Jesus Christ rather than obscure texts in the Bible or subjects like evolution or other religions. Establishing the deity of Christ opens the door to bring forth the claims of the New Testament. If Jesus was the Son of God, then what He said must be true. People like to discuss religion, politics and personalities, but they find it difficult to face Jesus Christ. Our job is to bring them face to face with the Savior — not with ourselves, our ideas or our church.

The children also need to be prepared in how to give a response to sincere but difficult questions about Christ. For example, can it really be proven that Jesus Christ died and literally rose from the dead? There are some good books and pamphlets you can give your children for resources such as Josh McDowell's *Evidence That Demands a Verdict* (volumes 1 and 2), Norman Anderson's *The Evidence for the Resurrection* and Frank Morison's *Who Moved the Stone?*[1] If the resurrection can be proven, then we establish His deity, opening the door to present our audience with the claims of Christ. Our experience has been that children are very interested in this type of material and can learn much from using it in their witnessing strategies.

This chapter has been a challenge to you, the leader or parent, to prepare yourselves to minister to children. You cannot just settle for being a good babysitter or activities coordinator. You need to have spiritual authority to lead the soldiers of God's army into battle. In the next chapter we will tell you more about how to teach youngsters to pray and evangelize.

CHAPTER FOUR

MOBILIZING CHILDREN FOR PRAYER AND EVANGELISM

Children and teenagers often limit their prayer experience to a few short minutes of praying over meals or special prayer requests while planning some fun endeavor. Their prayers often go like this:

Dear Lord, it's my birthday next week. Please make it possible for my parents to buy me that bicycle that I want so badly, and let it not rain during my party.

Or:

Lord, please give us a good sunny day when we go to the beach tomorrow, and make Becky's mother let her come. And may we have a real fun time.

Although these prayers are legitimate, they tend to be what we would call the selfish prayer. We need to encourage our youngsters to know what it means to really travail in prayer for the lost and to pray in the Holy Spirit (Jude 20). They must learn how to intercede for others (Eph. 6:18). Most children are naturally selfish, so the amount of spiritual power and training we put into their lives will result in the same amount of sacrificial living in them (Gal. 6:7). Sacrifice won't happen by accident.

A pastor's wife in Florida, Esther Ilnisky, has had children in all-night prayer meetings with amazing results. She is currently working on a project for the AD 2000 and Beyond movement to raise up one million children across the globe to pray for the children of the world. (For further information write to the Esther Network International, 854 Conniston Road, West Palm Beach, FL 33405 or call (407) 832-6490.)

Most youngsters have many friends and acquaintances who are either non-Christians or are not walking with the Lord. They have tremendous opportunities every day to share Christ with them. We suggest that you organize your youngsters into "witnessing teams." As they work together and support each other in prayer, they will see results that they never dreamed possible (James 5:16-18; Mark 11:24).

Children should be encouraged to write down on a sheet of paper a list of those people God has placed on their hearts to pray for. That way they can pray consistently for their salvation and ask God for the boldness to share the gospel with them. When the children are at school or in the neighborhood, they will realize that they are not alone but part of an army of young prayer warriors who are agreeing with them for their friends to be saved.

The importance of prayer-backing reminds me of a story I was told long ago. I believe it happened in China. An elder from a church had to take a large sum of money to another church. He had to travel on foot across a mountainous region which was frequented by bandits. The church could only spare two of their members for the mission, but the rest of the congregation prayed for a safe journey.

The men got through with no problems. Some time later the elder had to go to the hospital for a toe operation. In the ward he began to tell the patient next to him about his journey through the mountains. "I know all about it," said the man. "I was one of the bandits along that road. We could not attack you because there were too many of you."

"What do you mean?" the church elder asked. "There were only two of us."

"No, there were fourteen of you," he said. Some time later the church leader found out that the group at church which had been praying for them consisted of twelve persons. Add the two men who actually went on the journey, and that makes fourteen!

Each time the children meet together, have them give a progress report on their endeavors to reach their friends with the gospel. With an ongoing report, intelligent prayer and a spiritual strategy, much can be accomplished. It is better for them to concentrate on one or two people and keep after them until they have made a decision rather than to talk once to a large number of people. Perseverance is the name of the game!

Show the children that these principles are warfare tactics and should be taken very seriously (Matt. 10:16). Satan will be very active against these believing children. He will try to bring discouragement and fear. Many youngsters have reported back the first time with great excitement about how they talked to a friend about the Lord and made good progress. But often the next report they give on the follow-up is that the friend is avoiding them or is not interested in continuing the discussion.

In most cases the children's friends are not really reacting negatively. The devil is just trying to trick the child and stop him from continuing to witness. If he witnesses just once and doesn't persevere, the seeker will not take him seriously or will feel that the matters they are discussing are not of great importance. Witnessing should always be done in earnest. The young soldiers must always be willing and ready to pray with or for their friends. The Canadian mounted police philosophy is a good pattern to follow: 1) go after your man, 2) track him down, 3) capture him, 4) bring him back.

Strategies for School Evangelism

When you think of places where young people can spread the gospel, the first one that often comes to mind is the schools. From media reports in past years, you may have the impression that students are limited in their freedom to witness to other students on school property.

But this is not true! Students do not lose their constitutional rights when they go to school. Informal, non-disruptive witnessing can take place during free time in places such as the playground, lunch room, athletic facilities or hallways. Even elementary-age students can do this.[1]

Students in high school can also organize their own clubs for Bible study and prayer. That right was reaffirmed by a Supreme Court ruling in the summer of 1990. It stated that Bible clubs and prayer groups must be allowed to meet on high school campuses in the same facilities in which other noncurriculum-related clubs are allowed to meet. The key is that students must request and direct the meetings themselves. Teachers are not permitted to participate. The students can invite outside speakers to the meetings occasionally but not regularly.[2]

Groups such as the Fellowship of Christian Athletes can often obtain permission from school officials to use school facilities for meetings. (Christian unions were the equivalent to this in English secular schools.) A faculty advisor is usually required to be present.

Many children who attend secular schools complain that they are the only Christians in their school. This is not usually true. If one believer will become bold enough to organize a Christian meeting, he or she will be surprised to see how many other Christian young people will come out of hiding and get involved in the activities of a Christian club or Bible study.

When I started speaking at Christian meetings in secular schools in England, the attendance was usually only twelve or fifteen. However, that number grew to about 140 after a few months. Many of the youngsters involved became very bold and excited, and many of the students and teachers at the school were saved and healed.

Students will be attracted to your meetings if the speakers or discussions address current areas of interest such as AIDS, drug abuse, premarital sex or pornography. This will give an opportunity for the gospel to be preached in a relevant fashion as it relates to these subjects.

Pitfalls to Avoid

We must also be alerted to the dangers which can arise when young people are involved in personal witnessing. Satan is out to destroy their effectiveness. Personal witnessing between members of the opposite sex — especially among the older children and teens — should be taken over by a member of the witnessing team who is of the same sex. If a youngster becomes emotionally involved with someone of the opposite sex (especially an unbeliever), they are putting themselves in the danger zone and opening themselves up to deception. They will eventually lose their effectiveness for the Lord (2 Cor. 6:14-18).

It is not uncommon for a person to fake being a Christian just to stay involved with or marry a believer. If the Christian falls for this ploy, the end result is almost always tragic. Young people should always resist trade-offs such as, "I'll come with you to church if you will come with me to a party." However, a youth could go to a secular party if he or she could bring the whole team and use the party as a mission field.

Youngsters should always be ready to call in a more experienced Christian to help them with their soul-winning endeavors. If one of the young people reaches a certain stage in sharing the gospel with someone but then seems to get stuck, that is often the time to call in reinforcements from the witnessing team. These youngsters must remember that this is a team effort.

All Kinds of Evangelism

We've already discussed witnessing at school, but there are many other types of evangelism in which children can get involved: street witnessing, door-to-door witnessing, open-air preaching, one-on-one witnessing, revival and crusade counseling, hospital ministry, literature evangelism and youth clubs.

Another option for teenagers is to go to a foreign country with their church group for a couple of weeks and participate in a church outreach. However, for some reason it always seems easier to evangelize overseas than it does right in our own backyard. We believe that God wants our young people to be effective in their own towns and neighborhoods and among their own peers.

Those who are leading the children, then, must set a good example. We cannot be like the stern sergeant who said, "Don't do as I do; do as I say!" Those in leadership must be willing to go out with these youngsters and be an active part of evangelism. Witnessing at the beach, in the streets or on campuses must be done with adult supervision. A good place for informal witnessing is where young people congregate at particular restaurants, video game arcades, sports fields, theaters, swimming pools or malls.

About a year ago we were doing a weekend seminar in a church in Los Angeles. After the Sunday meeting the children asked if they could go out witnessing in the local park. The pastor agreed, and a couple of the children's workers took them out witnessing after lunch. The children had a great time sharing with other children who were on the playground and even witnessed to a number of the adults. They ended up praying for several children to receive salvation.

Another type of evangelism that has been popular and successful over the years is taking neighborhood children to local churches by bus. Much of this has concentrated on encouraging children to bring other children. With the right vision and training, bus ministry can bring in more than numbers. It can be a means to see children saved and trained as a part of God's young army. If children are taught that being a soldier means they must be obedient at home, keep their rooms tidy, offer to help around the house and not be mean to their brothers and sisters, they will then bring their parents into the kingdom!

Sensitivity to Parents

Sometimes unsaved parents react negatively if their children come home from a Christian meeting and claim they have been saved. The parents may have all sorts of fears that their children are being brainwashed by religious fanatics. They may forbid them to come anymore, or even bring complaints or threats to the youth pastor.

To try to prevent this from happening, it would be a good idea to have tactful letters or audio-tapes to give to newly saved children. These tapes can be given to their parents in order to establish the validity of the church involved. The tapes can also point out the problems that children and teens face today, such as drugs, crime and sexual promiscuity. Finally, the tapes would assure the parents that the church will help the parents raise their children by imparting to their young-sters the positive principles found in the Bible such as faith, honesty, peace, love, purity — and especially the teachings of Jesus Christ.

The youth pastor could also offer to meet with the parents to put their minds at rest and to as-sure them that their child has shown an active interest in the Christian faith. He could ask the parents' permission to continue to help in the de-velopment of their child's spiritual and moral wel-fare without undermining the parents' authority. He could also offer to work with them closely, in-forming them regularly of the progress being made.

Letting Children Lead Their Own Meetings

Many church meetings for teenagers are run solely by the adults. All responsibility is in their hands and the youth are just considered specta-tors. If this happens, the kids will first resent it and then lose interest in any spiritual endeavor. Finally they will just want to know what kind of fun things are being planned for them. They will expect everything to be handed to them on a silver platter.

As we have mentioned previously, an army has lower-ranking officers who have a certain degree of responsibility but still submit to those of higher rank. Likewise, children can be given places of authority and responsibility if they are being discipled and encouraged by the leaders. They will soon rise to become effective in the work of the ministry.

On the other hand, one must remember that children are still children — they are not fully mature. That means they can move in God's anointing and let His power flow through them in one meeting, and then in another they misbehave. You may even find them squabbling with one another just after such a powerful time of ministry.

The work of the Holy Spirit is twofold: to anoint or impart power (Luke 2:40, Gal. 5:22-23) and to develop character or the fruit of the Spirit (Acts 2:17-18, 1:8; Luke 4:18). Our children need to learn to yield daily to the Spirit within them. The anointing can come instantly and then be lost again if they get into the flesh. As they mature in God through the inward working of the Holy Spirit, they will experience a more continual anointing.

Charles Spurgeon read books on theology at eleven, preached at fifteen, pastored at seventeen and pastored the largest church in England at nineteen — the Metropolitan Tabernacle of London. The church was closed for expansion and he moved into the famous Crystal Palace and drew crowds of ten thousand. Many London preachers were upset that a young kid should be allowed to pastor such a church.[3] But his age didn't seem to dissuade the Holy Spirit.

In Indonesia children took part in a great move of the Spirit in the 1960s. Youngsters between the ages of eight and twelve worked signs and wonders and preached the gospel. The late David duPlessis, a Pentecostal leader who held worldwide respect, prophesied that this was just a foretaste of the way God would use children in the last days to bring revival (Acts 2:17-18; Luke 2:40-47).[4]

A number of years ago when we lived in England, we were ministering to a teenager named Nigel. He was involved with the youth group at the local evangelical church but was hungry for the baptism of the Holy Spirit. When we prayed for him, he suddenly began to bounce in the chair. He bounced in the chair and then all around the room, saying, "Bubbity, bubbity, bubbity."

That doesn't sound like the Holy Spirit, I thought. But in that moment Nigel had become a firebrand for God. The power of God swept through his youth group until the pastor asked him to leave. (Nigel's church was very suspicious of charismatics.) He led Christian meetings at the secular school he attended and invited us to come and preach. A revival broke out in the school, and the meetings grew from a handful to a group of 150 or more. He eventually went to Bristol University and arranged for us to come and preach to the students there. The last report we heard about Nigel was that he was an elder in a growing church!

Recently a little eight-year-old girl named Zoe

was greatly moved in a children's meeting in which we were ministering. Full of faith, she went downstairs to the adults' meeting and immediately laid her hands on a man in a wheelchair. The man had been crippled for five years, but he leaped out of the wheelchair!

About three years ago we were ministering in a Word of Faith church in Orlando, Florida. We had seen God move on little children, and in one meeting about twenty of them were piled up on the stage under the power of the Holy Spirit. Kevin, the pastor's son, who was about fifteen at the time, was sitting in the back of the meeting with the rest of the teenagers, simply observing, but trying not to get involved.

He told us later that when he saw a little seven-year-old swaying under the power of God and later falling, he thought to himself: "If I stood there would the same thing happen to me?" So Kevin moved the little boy aside and stood on the very same spot. Immediately a fire came down his right arm and hand to his chest and then up his left arm and hand. Then it moved back down to his chest. He was transformed in that instant and became a radical for God!

The following Sunday Kevin preached to the whole church for about fifteen minutes, weeping for the lost and exhorting the church to have a burden for evangelism. His father called me a year or so later and reported that Kevin had gone to Bible college to prepare for the ministry. Those revival meetings had been the instrument that changed his life!

We have seen through these testimonies that children can not only minister to one another during their meetings, but they can also minister to the adults. Our children need to know that they are not second-class citizens in the kingdom of God. They are not just imitating their parents by going to church. They have great potential in God. Acts 10:34 tells us that God is no respecter of persons — and we believe that includes persons of all ages.

Paying the Price

To see an army of children empowered by the Holy Spirit and reaching other youngsters for God will be costly. The entire church — including the adults and especially the parents — must be willing to pay the price. Family life-styles will have to be adjusted. Television, recreation, extra school activities, sports and amusements will have to take second place. A commitment to making God's kingdom the first priority will have to be established (Matt. 6:33). Loving Jesus must come before business, pleasure and the cares of this life.

Our children may be regarded by some as abnormal. They will not spend their time flirting, dating, going to movies and partying. They will be seriously dedicated to God's purposes (Matt. 6:19-21; Eph. 5:1-5). Not every child or parent will respond to the discipline and commitment necessary to achieve God's highest calling. Many teenagers will want to know just how much they can get away with and still remain a Christian. But when they receive a real salvation experience, they will want to know what they can do to get to know God in a closer way (Phil. 3:10).

Many years ago in England we held Friday night youth outreach meetings in our town. We trained the youngsters for evangelism in Saturday morning discipleship classes. Then in the afternoons they would go out into the town with guitars and sing and witness to shoppers. In the evening we would take them downtown to witness outside the bars.

Many of the customers were too scared to go in or come out because they knew the "Jesus freaks" were in town. Twelve-year-olds were receiving words of knowledge (1 Cor. 12:8) and witnessing to the bar customers. Some of the leading drug pushers were saved through that endeavor and are leaders in churches today! The youngsters also had a tremendous effect on the local schools by praying and witnessing to their friends. Many children were saved and healed.

During that time none of these children were concerned with dating and flirting. They had more important things to do. They had the assurance that God had the right marriage partner picked out for them at the right time, and they did not have to experiment with numerous boyfriends or girlfriends to discover His choice for them. They just trusted God and went about the business of the kingdom.

The Catalyst for Action

I remember having the privilege of addressing several hundred youth and children's ministers at a Sunday school teachers' convention in England a few years ago.

After the meeting a couple who led a youth

group in a local church asked me how they could encourage their youngsters to pray more freely in public. They said the teenagers were very inhibited, and after many weeks they had only been able to get one or two of them to pray short prayers in public. I told them it might be a case of putting the cart before the horse. I believed that they needed to pray and believe for a mighty baptism of the Holy Spirit to fall on the youth, and then they would not be able to stop them from praying.

I encouraged them to concentrate on the Holy Spirit and His power, and to pray and believe for the anointing to come. That should always be our first priority, and then all the other concerns will fall into place. Those leaders also needed to be free in prayer themselves and on fire for God so that they could inspire their youngsters.

Appropriately, this chapter began and is ending with instructions about prayer. The prayers of children and teenagers need to do more than thank God for food and request some little favors. The youth need to intercede for the salvation of those around them. Let them pray for healings and gifts of the Spirit as God gives them faith. When their prayer life is strong, send them out for the harvest at their schools, in the streets and so on. As converts are made, be sensitive to the concerns of the parents. Finally, the youth should not just be spectators, but should be used as leaders during their meetings.

In the final chapter of this book we are going to look at one of the most exciting aspects of ministering to young people — releasing them in the power of the Spirit.

CHAPTER FIVE

RELEASING CHILDREN IN THE HOLY SPIRIT'S POWER

We have seen a number of children delivered from demons over the years. If you tell parents that their child needs deliverance, they often get alarmed and upset. It's like telling them that their child has fleas!

Children can be affected by demonic activity in several ways. The Bible says that the sins of the fathers are visited upon the children unto the third and fourth generations (Num. 14:18). Many of our children could have inherited sinful habits, curses or the effects of false or occult religions from their forefathers. They need to be cut off spiritually from the heredity of the family tree. If the parents have problems with fear, anger, stubbornness and so on, then the children again may need deliverance.

Often you may pray for deliverance for small

children while they are asleep. Even though their minds are not aware of what is happening, their spirits are. It is important that infants are raised in a loving, humorous and godly atmosphere. When they are old enough to understand, it will be so easy for them to make a committment to Christ. A church nursery should be more than changing diapers and holding bottles. It should be a real ministry to the spirits of infants.[1]

Often things like fear, lust, violence, rebellion and so on can come as youngsters watch certain television programs. Things left around the house, such as occult literature, pornography, certain record albums, pagan images, Freemasonry regalia* or occult paraphernalia will also hinder the youngster's spiritual progress.

A number of years ago some friends of ours called us over to their house. Their small infant was waking up every night screaming in terror. We eventually searched the baby's bedroom and found a walking stick. It was made of black ebony wood and had a bird's head on it with strange carvings all over it. I believe it came from India. We took it out and burned it, and from that day on the baby had no more trouble sleeping (Acts 19:18-19).

If we want to be filled with the Holy Spirit, we often have to be emptied first of the garbage we have accumulated or inherited. Some denominations do not believe that Christians can have de-

---

* Freemasonry is a fraternal organization that practices secret rituals and has occultic origins. For more information see "The Power Behind Freemasonry" by Lee Grady in the June 1990 issue of *Charisma & Christian Life*.

mons. They argue, "How can a Christian be demon possessed? Even more so, how can such a thing happen to a Christian *child*?"

We are not talking about demon possession. We are talking about people and youngsters *possessing* demons or spirits. In theory, if all Christians were totally filled with the Holy Spirit as Christ was, then it would be impossible to "possess" any demons. But we deal with many people, including youngsters, who are Spirit-filled by doctrinal persuasion rather than experience.

We have found that people (including children) sometimes manifest demons when the Holy Spirit is moving in a meeting. It appears that the power of God often stirs these demons up and agitates them, as with the Gadarene man (Mark 5:1-8). Sometimes when people come to our meetings from dead religious churches, they have to be delivered from religious spirits or even Freemasonry spirits. If children have been raised in that kind of environment, you can imagine what their needs must be.

Learning to Wait on God

The moving of the Spirit in all of our gatherings is essential. I have known of many children's and youth meetings where there has been no moving of the Spirit, and the presence of the supernatural was completely lacking.

We know that Christianity is not just religious psychology, philosophy and teaching. It is the power of God. This power must be evident in our lives and meetings. Not only are we to believe by faith for the supernatural in our meetings, but we must also teach our children to move in the gifts after they have received the baptism of the Holy Spirit.

In regard to teaching children to move out in the gifts, the following examples should be an encouragement. Since the restoration of the prophetic ministry, a number of churches have special meetings from time to time called a presbytery. A traditional presbytery is comprised of the body of leaders for congregations within a certain area. In a prophetic presbytery, recognized prophets come to a church and minister to the elders, the ministers, the church staff and the congregation. They give prophetic confirmation, direction and insight into future ministries. Often members of the church who have a prophetic calling are allowed to participate under the jurisdiction of the recognized prophets.

We were ministering at a conference in Michigan and ended up having a prophetic presbytery with the children. As I began to prophesy over the children, two or three of these youngsters, who were about nine to eleven years of age, joined me and also began to prophesy.

During a visit to a charismatic church in Gainesville, Florida, the Holy Spirit fell on many of the children in a children's meeting. They were then invited to the adult meeting to testify about what had happened to them. They concluded by prophesying and giving words of knowledge to the adults for about an hour.

I can only draw one conclusion from the experiences I have just shared: Our children must know that the Holy Spirit is given to them so they can move in the supernatural realm. They also need to realize that through their Spirit baptism they receive power and boldness for witnessing.

One of the hallmarks of our meetings is our dependency on the Holy Spirit. We instruct the youngsters and adults to be quiet and still before the Lord. Many Christians, even Christian leaders, do not know how to wait on the Holy Spirit in a meeting. We are always in a hurry, and those of us who are more outgoing and verbal tend to jump in right away and play the role of the Holy Spirit.

We ask the people to get their minds off everything except the Lord, to open themselves up and ask the Holy Spirit to come and possess them. That can be a little scary for some people. People think of demon possession, but not Holy Spirit possession. They think of having the Holy Spirit but not of the Holy Spirit having them. As we bring them to the place of faith, God always moves by His Spirit.

For example, I once encountered a resistant group of teenagers at a youth crusade in Ohio. After my sermon in the final meeting, I asked about fifteen teenagers at the back of the church to come forward so I could pray for them. Many other teens were there, but these were the ones who really did not want to be at the meeting. They were all backsliders. They came onto the platform, and I prayed for God's power to fall on them. I told them to wait for God to move, and then I sat down on the sixth row next to the pastor.

Five minutes passed by, and nothing happened. Ten minutes passed and still nothing. Fifteen minutes passed, and by this time the youngsters were standing there looking and feeling very sheepish. Then after about twenty minutes the power of God fell on a young girl. She began weeping and speaking in tongues, and then she laid hands on the rest of the youngsters and prayed for them. The Spirit began to move all over them, and then He began to move among the entire church. Children were laughing, crying, getting healed and rejoicing. Many said to me, "I did not want to come to that meeting, but my parents made me. Now I'm glad they did, because I wouldn't have missed it for the world."

This moving of the Spirit lasted two hours, and I just sat beside the pastor and watched. I did not do anything. He said to me afterward, "You know, if that had been me and nothing had happened after five minutes, I would have closed the meeting. My! How we need to learn how to wait on God!"

All Things Are Possible With Your Children

When our eldest daughter, Faith, was about nine or ten years old, she began to get violent pains in her chest. When she complained of the pain, my wife Kathie said, "Is the Lord saying something to you?" (She felt it was a spiritual sign rather than a physical problem.)

Faith replied, "I keep thinking of that Christian man Ron, who has been to our house a couple of times." My wife then suggested that they pray in the Spirit for him for a while. After they prayed, the pain left. A few days later the same thing happened, and Faith prayed for Ron again. Then about a week later it happened again, and

Faith prayed and felt a total release from the pain. She then had a sense that Ron would be fine.

Kathie decided to call Ron on the phone to see how he was doing. As she talked with him, he shared that about a year earlier he had experienced a heart attack, and the doctor had warned him about stress. Recently he had built three houses and was not able to sell them. He was under tremendous pressure to make the loan payments. He had started getting pains in his chest, but each time a peace had come upon him and the pain had left. It had happened on three occasions. Then God enabled him to sell the houses, and he felt fit as a fiddle.

Kathie shared with Ron how the Lord had used Faith, a nine-year-old girl, to intercede for him. In a sense she had been put in trust with his life. Although God could have used someone else if Faith had not responded, He does want to use children more than we think!

When we minister in churches and conventions, we usually have several meetings with the children; a training seminar with the youth pastors, parents and children's workers; and then a meeting with the whole assembly in which we release the children to minister in the power of the Holy Spirit. In the final meeting I quite often preach from the text found in 1 Corinthians 1:27-29:

> But God hath chosen the foolish things of the world to confound the wise; and God hath chosen the weak things of the world to confound the things which are

mighty; and base things of the world, and things which are despised, hath God chosen, yea, and things which are not, to bring to nought things that are; that no flesh should glory in his presence.

I encourage the children that God has chosen the foolish and the weak, the dummies and the nothings. I tell them that if God spoke through the mouth of a donkey, then there is hope for them — if they dare to believe! I explain that their strength is not in themselves but in the mighty power of the Holy Spirit. I tell them that when they acknowledge they are nothing and that they have no power or wisdom against the devil, then God makes Christ unto them wisdom, righteousness, sanctification and redemption. Therefore, they can be confident to boast — not in themselves — but in the Lord (1 Cor. 1:30-31).

I also explain to the children that the apostle Paul knew what it was to be weak and that he didn't rely on his own ability to work for God:

And I was with you in weakness, and in fear, and in much trembling. And my speech and my preaching was not with enticing words of man's wisdom, but in demonstration of the Spirit and of power (1 Cor. 2:3-4).

When I am weak, then am I strong (2 Cor. 12:10).

I tell them that even the Lord Jesus did not rely

on His own ability or power to fulfill His calling, but on the power of the Holy Spirit:

> The Son can do nothing of himself, but what he seeth the Father do (John 5:19).

I remind them that even though they are weak in themselves, God has armor that fits any size child so that they all can be mighty for Him (Eph. 6:10-18).

It is very important that we encourage our youngsters to be bold for God, and that we help to make opportunities for them to function spiritually in our church meetings and to witness for Christ in their schools and neighborhoods.

It would be a great shame if after reading this book one would just lay it aside and carry on doing the same old things in the same old way — not because these methods have been successful, but because they are convenient. We know that there is a price to pay for the anointing of the Holy Spirit. Input produces output, and we reap what we sow (Gal. 6:7).

If we have been using the same methods for years, and most other Christians have been using them with little or limited success, then it's time we changed and sowed something different in the lives of our children and our churches. Remember, God is no respecter of persons (Rom. 2:11; Acts 10:34). He only respects believers. In other words, it is not our children's ages that stop God from using them, only the quality of their believing. Many children think they are too young for God to use them, or they think that God does not expect them to be serious with Him at a young age.

Then there are adults who think they are too old for God to use them. Some people use a bad upbringing as an excuse for God to pass them by. "My mother was a drunk, and my father beat me, so I'm just one of those people who doesn't fit in with church folks." In essence they are saying that their weaknesses are stronger than God's ability to change them.

Summary

This has been a book about faith. We have seen and are still seeing God's Spirit move mightily among youngsters. When that happens, we are seeing Him move mightily on whole churches. A nationally known prophet, Bob Jones of Independence, Missouri, told me some time ago that Satan is attacking the church and attempting to rob people of childlike faith.

Can we really believe that little children and teenagers can be mighty for God in our day and our generation? Can we believe that a great army of youngsters will be raised up in churches across the nation to usher in a great end-time revival? The answer lies with us: "If thou canst believe, all things are possible to him that believeth" (Mark 9:23).

If some churches close their doors to a radical move of the Spirit and a revolutionary change in the children's program, then eventually God will move outside of those churches. Could it be that your church will miss God? We hope not.

Many leaders are fearful of things getting out of order in their church (1 Cor. 14:40), and so they believe that allowing children and teens to move out and minister could become an embarrassment. In the past the emphasis in the injunction in 1 Corinthians 14:40, "Let all things be done decently and in order," has been on "decently and in order." But if we were allowing "all things to be done," we would have something to put in order.

Another way of looking at this is found in Proverbs 14:4, "Where no oxen are, the crib is clean: but much increase is by the strength of the ox." If we desire just a clean crib, then we will not see the power of God move through the children. With children and adults, there is always the risk of getting the crib dirty with a fleshly or emotional display during a move of the Spirit. But if we accept the fact that there may be a mess here and there and not be overly concerned, we could experience revival.

EPILOGUE

Most parents who have had a hard struggle to succeed in this life do not want their children to go through the same hardships they experienced. They desire to see their children have the benefits and opportunities which they were deprived of in their youth. Many people have built a successful family business to pass on to their heirs. To give their children a better education, some property, an inheritance or a better start in life is the goal of many parents.

What about our children's spiritual inheritance? Many of us are not able to leave much to our children in terms of material wealth and security, but we can leave them a spiritual legacy. I was not saved until I was twenty-five, and it was ten years later before I was baptized in the Holy Spirit. Therefore, I had a late start in building my children's spiritual legacy.

My children have a tremendous advantage over me. They are moving in the power of God, hearing truths and receiving revelation that I knew nothing of when I was their age.

I tell my daughters that they are standing on my shoulders. They will be moving in a far greater anointing than I have ever done when they reach adulthood — if they do not despise their inheritance.

Our children must not throw away their spiritual posterity for a mess of pottage (Gen. 25:29-34). The things of the world are not to be compared with the kingdom of God. Don't offer your children religion or phony Christianity. If all we have is dead church-going — or even lively church-going, with a dead personal Christian life — then our children will reject what we have.

We do not believe it is necessary or even to be expected that our children will backslide and go into the world to taste its pleasures after they have reached their late teens or early twenties. There is a belief that many young people need to experience the world's ways before they realize that Christ is the answer, but one doesn't have to drink the bottle to find out it contains poison.

Neither do we expect our kids to end up being nominal in their Christianity, just making an occasional appearance at church to please their parents, or to give themselves a kind of minimal spiritual insurance policy. As parents we must impart to them a rich inheritance. So it behooves us to make sure we have the real thing. Our children are to be children of destiny. Let us give them a head start.

NOTES

Chapter 1

1. Charles Spurgeon, *Come, Ye Children* (Pasadena, Tex.: Pilgrim Publications, 1974).

2. Sunday-morning sermon by Dr. Martyn Lloyd-Jones at Westminster Chapel in London, England, in the mid-1960s.

Chapter 2

1. Glen Doman, *How to Multiply Your Baby's Intelligence* (Garden City, N.Y.: Doubleday and Company, Inc., 1984).

2. James Stewart, *Invasion of Wales* (Asheville, N.C.: Revival Literature, 1963).

3. Robert E. Coleman, *One Divine Moment* (Old Tappan, N.J.: Fleming Revell, Spire Books, 1970).

4. Owen Murphy, *When God Stepped Down From Heaven* (Grandville, Mo.: Kansas City Fellowship, 1988).

5. Joshua Bradley, *Accounts of Religious Revivals in Many Parts of the United States* (reprint, Wheaton, Ill.: Richard Owen Roberts Publisher, 1980).

6. Eva Stuart Watt, *Floods on Dry Ground* (London and Edinburgh: Marshall, Morgan, and Scott, 1939).

7. R. Bradley Jones, *Rent Heavens* (Asheville, N.C.: Revival Literature, 1950).

8. G.A. Rawlyk, *Ravished by the Spirit* (Kingston, Ontario, and Montreal, Quebec: McGill-Queens University Press, 1984).

9. *Ibid.*

10. R.G. Moyles, *The Blood and Fire in Canada* (Toronto: Peter Martin Associates, Ltd., 1977).

11. Lindley Baldwin, *Samuel Morris (The Ebony Saint)* (Minneapolis, Minn.: Bethany House Publishers, 1987).

12. H.A. Baker, *Visions Beyond the Veil* (Springdale, Pa.: Whitaker House, 1973).

Chapter 3

1. Josh McDowell, *Evidence That Demands a Verdict*, vols. 1 and 2 (San Bernardino, Calif.: Here's Life Publishers, 1979); J.N.D. Anderson, *The Evidence for the Resurrection* (Downers Grove, Ill.: InterVarsity Press, 1979); Frank Morison, *Who Moved the Stone?* (Grand Rapids, Mich.: Zondervan, 1979).

Chapter 4

1. Jay Sekulow, *From Intimidation to Victory* (Lake Mary, Fla.: Creation House, 1990), chapter 5, "Purging Christianity From the Schools."

2. More helpful information can also be found in the appendix of Sekulow's book (see previous note). If you need further help you can contact C.A.S.E. (Christian Advocates Serving Evangelism), P.O. Box 450349, Atlanta, GA 30345.

3. Arnold Dallimore, *Spurgeon: A New Biography* (Carlisle, Pa: Banner of Truth, 1987).

4. DuPlessis made the statement during a Christian Caribbean cruise in 1976, according to Pastor Chuck Call of Tabb, Virginia. For more exciting reports about the way God worked through children in the Indonesian revival, read Mel Tari and Cliff Dudley's *Like a Mighty Wind* (Green Forest, Ark.: New Leaf Press, 1978).

Chapter 5

1. Jacqueline G. Coons, *Forbid Them Not: Supernaturally Ministering to Infants* (Flint, Mich.: Faith Fellowship Publications, 1983).

MATERIALS AVAILABLE FROM GOOD NEWS FELLOWSHIP MINISTRIES

Books

The Armor of God
A children's Bible study based on Ephesians 6:10-18
(illustrated). By David Walters

Equipping the Younger Saints
A guide for teaching children about spiritual gifts.
By David Walters

Fact or Fantasy
A study on Christian apologetics designed for
children (illustrated). By David Walters

Deliverance for Children and Teens
How demons enter and take advantage of innocent,
vulnerable children. By Bill Banks

Forbid Them Not
A guide for ministering supernaturally to infants.
Especially designed for mothers and nursery workers.
By Jacqueline G. Coons

Perfected Praise
The steps for leading children into meaningful
worship. By Richard Malm

Samuel Morris
The amazing story of a fifteen-year-old boy who
was saved in a Christian mission after escaping
from a hostile tribe in the African jungle.
This fast-paced book tells how he was used
by God in America. By Lindley Baldwin

Soldiers With Little Feet
The author writes: "I want to see the children
rise up to be ministering little members
of the body of Christ." This is a great follow-up
to *Kids in Combat.* By Dian Layton

Visions Beyond the Veil
An account of supernatural manifestations
of the Holy Spirit among small children
in a Chinese mission. By H.A. Baker

Videotapes

All Rapped Up
An inside look at the rap/dance music scene.
By Eric Holmberg with Reel to Real Ministries

Hell's Bells
An exposé of the dangers of rock 'n' roll. A five-tape
series. By Eric Holmberg with Reel to Real Ministries

The Bride
A musical and dramatic presentation of the
church as Christ's bride. Children love it.
By Reba Rambo and Dony McGuire

For current pricing write:

Good News Fellowship Ministries
Route 28, Box 95-D
Sleepy Creek Road
Macon, GA 31210
(912) 757-8071
(912) 757-0136 FAX

ABOUT THE WALTERS FAMILY

David and Kathie Walters are originally from England. They spent eleven years under the ministry of the famous expository preacher Dr. Martyn Lloyd-Jones of London. After being baptized in the Holy Spirit in 1969, they experienced a revival in their hometown. A church grew out of their home meetings, and they started to travel, evangelizing in schools, colleges and universities throughout the country.

They also visited many churches and brought a move of the Holy Spirit to them. The pages of this book present their twenty years of ministering on the anointing of God to youth pastors, Sunday school teachers, children, young adults and parents. David and Kathie presently reside in Macon, Georgia, with their two daughters.

For booking information, write or call:

Good News Fellowship Ministries
Route 28, Box 95-D
Sleepy Creek Road
Macon, GA 31210
(912) 757-8071
(912) 757-0136 FAX

RAISING A GENERATION OF ANOINTED CHILDREN AND YOUTH

ONE-DAY TRAINING SEMINAR

*Equipping Parents, Youth Pastors,
Sunday School Teachers and
Children's Workers*

The churches in your area can experience
one of these dynamic seminars. Author and
speaker David Walters imparts a fresh
vision and anointing to parents and to those
who work with children and youth. Walters says:

Children do not have a baby or junior Holy Spirit!

*Children are baptized in the Holy Spirit
to do much more than play, be entertained
or listen to a few moral object lessons!*

*The average church-wise child can be
turned around and set on fire for God!*

*Christian teenagers do not have to surrender to peer
pressure — they can become the peers!*

David Walters has written a number
of books, including:

Kids in Combat
The Armor of God
Fact or Fantasy
Equipping the Younger Saints

A number of his articles have been
published in magazines such as
Ministries Today and in
CharismaLife Learning Resources.
"Preparing Our Children for the Nineties"
is the title of one of his recent articles.

If you would like to receive further
information about sponsoring
a seminar for your area, write:

Good News Fellowship Ministries
Route 28, Box 95-D
Sleepy Creek Road
Macon, GA 31210

or call

(912) 757-8071
(912) 757-0136 FAX